JN094428

企業と社会フォーラム学会誌　第9号

サステナビリティ人材の育成と経営教育

編集：企業と社会フォーラム　　　発行：千倉書房

目　次

は じ め に

　企業と社会フォーラム（JFBS）学会誌第9号は，「サステナビリティ人材の育成と経営教育」を
テーマとした昨年の第9回年次大会での議論を踏まえ，その後の研究成果，さらに投稿論文などを
加え構成されている。

　過去20年ほどの間にCSRは重要な経営課題として認識されるようになったと同時に，研究・教
育課題としてもグローバルに広がり，新しいマインドセットをもった研究者や実務家の育成が求め
られるようになってきた。プライベートな企業が国内外の社会的課題に取り組むことには無理があ
る，あるいは取り組むべきではないと長らく考えられてきたが，企業に求められる役割・責任が変
わり，今やビジネスのもつ強み（技術力，ブランド力，ネットワーク力など）がそういった課題の解
決に貢献するという認識が広がり，さらにサステナビリティ・マインドをもった人材の育成が求め
られるようになってきた。

　サステナビリティという視点は，企業経営のあり方や教育に新しいビジョンを提示していくポテ
ンシャルをもっている。CSR，サステナビリティの課題に取り組んでいくに当たっては，複雑にか
かわりあう経済・社会・環境の課題にトータルにアプローチする発想が求められる。とくに今回の
ような新型コロナウイルスが企業社会につきつけたさまざまな課題にどう対応し，持続可能な社会
をつくっていくか。SDGsブームを越えて，それらを踏まえた新しいシステムを構築していく必要
に迫られている。こういったマインドをもつサステナビリティ人材の育成には，従来のマネジメン
トスキルの教育にとどまらず，幅広くステイクホルダーと議論を行っていくことが期待されてい
る。しかしながら，日本ではまだそういった認識が定着しているとは言えない。

　国際的にサステナビリティへの関心が高まる中，多くの国の大学・ビジネススクールには実務界
から責任あるリーダーシップと高い倫理意識をもった卒業生を育てることが期待されている。ビジ
ネス教育の国際認証AACSBは，今や各ビジネススクールにその教育・研究においてCSR関連の
課題に取り組むことを求めている。また責任ある経営教育原則PRMEは，国連グローバルコンパ
クトを踏まえた責任ある企業経営をリードするビジネスリーダーを育てることを使命とした組織
で，700を超える大学，ビジネススクールが調印している。日本ではまだこうした国際的な取り組
みはあまり理解されていない。CSR/サステナビリティ教育は，大学と企業，国際機関，NGOな
どが協力しながら取り組み，ローカル/グローバルな課題の解決に貢献していく人材を育成してい
くことが求められている。

　こうした課題について議論するため，企業と社会フォーラム第9回年次大会が2019年9月5日
（木），6日（金）の2日間にわたり早稲田大学にて開催された。今大会にも日本のみならず，ドイ
ツ，スペイン，オーストラリア，タイ，台湾，中国，バングラデシュ，香港から，学界，産業界，
労働界，NPO/NGOなど各セクターにわたり多くの参加者が集まった。中でも，アジアを拠点に
サステナブル経済の構築に取り組むB Corp AsiaとJFBSの連携によって，30名の訪問団がタイ，
台湾から参加し，特別セッションも開催された。それぞれの立場からサステナビリティ人材の育成

について多面的な議論が繰り広げられた。

　大会はドイツの Cologne Business School にて学長を務める Elisabeth Fröhlich 教授，およびグローバル・コンパクト・ネットワーク・ジャパン代表理事の有馬利男氏による基調講演，それに引き続いての全体セッションから始まった。企画セッションでは「企業における『ビジネスと人権』教育・研修の課題」，「Sustainability Leadership Training」，「Higher Education for Sustainability」，「サステナビリティ人材の育成におけるメディアの役割」をテーマに，企業，大学，メディアなど各機関が進める具体的取り組みの紹介とパネルディスカッションが行われた。

　自由論題報告セッションでは「Sustainability in Management Education」，「日本企業の CSR 経営」，「Global B Corp Movement and Asia Development」，「CSR Management」などのセッションに分かれて，全部で22本の研究報告・ケース報告がなされ，活発な議論・交流が行われた。

　本大会では福川恭子（一橋大学大学院教授），Schmidpeter, René（Professor, Cologne Business School, Germany），谷本寛治（早稲田大学教授）がプログラム委員会を構成し，大会プログラムの立案，自由論題報告および Doctoral Workshop のプロポーザルの審査，企画セッションの司会などを担当した。

　本学会誌にはこの年次大会のテーマに関する「イントロダクション」，さらに「招待論文（論文および事例紹介・解説）」，「投稿論文（論文および事例紹介・解説）」が収められている。投稿論文に関しては，JFBS 編集委員会（委員長 國部克彦神戸大学教授）による審査（double-blind review）が行われ，今回は投稿された7本の論文のうち2本が掲載されることとなった。今後も積極的な投稿を願っている。

　さて，次回第10回年次大会では，「サーキュラーエコノミーを目指して」（Circular Economy Transition: Exploring the Institutional, Organizational & Behavioral Dimensions）をテーマとして議論を行う。これまでビジネスは，生産—消費—廃棄と直線的に展開するリニアなモデルで行われてきた。しかしこの伝統的な産業モデルでは，もはや持続可能な経済社会を実現することはできない。資源獲得から生産，輸送，エネルギー消費，廃棄のプロセスと経済成長を切り離して議論していては，循環型経済（サーキュラーエコノミー）に移行していくことは不可能である。サーキュラーエコノミーに向けた理論構築，そして実現可能な政府の政策や企業における経営戦略の策定，さらにセクターを超えたコラボレーションが求められており，本大会において広く議論する予定である。具体的には，プラスチック問題，食品ロス，サステナブルファッション，再生可能エネルギー，持続可能な農業，シェアリングなど，多くの課題がある。

　本来であれば，この大会は 2020 年 9 月 4〜5 日に開催される予定であったが，新型コロナウイルスの影響により1年延期し，2021 年 9 月初めに開催することとなった。同感染症の一日も早い収束を願うともに，多くの研究者，実務家が再び集まり，活発な議論が再開できることを願っている。大会の内容や申し込みについては，JFBS のウエブサイトを参照いただきたい https://j-fbs.

jp/。

　最後に，今号も発行に当たっては千倉書房に大変お世話になった。記して感謝の意を表したい。

2020 年 6 月

企業と社会フォーラム会長
早稲田大学商学学術院商学部教授

谷本　寛治

Japan Forum of Business and Society Annals, No.9. pp. 1–19, 2020   1

(Re) thinking Education for Sustainable Development: A Capability Approach

Kyoko Fukukawa

Professor, School of Business Administration, Hitotsubashi Universiy

Key words : Education for sustainable development, Capability approach, Responsible management education

【Abstract】

The paper examines the significance of Education for Sustainability Development (ESD) within the context of business studies in Higher Education. Adopting Amartya Sen's Capability Approach, the paper argues for 'sustainability' as the underlying capability *of* ESD, not simply its goal. This gives rise to what Sen refers to as 'evaluative space', whereby we understand how actions within one domain impacts upon other domains. Current practices in implementing ESD can lead to a decoupling of practice and rhetoric. Yet, by extending the evaluative space (or the array of factors and outcomes) we can seek greater consensus with business and wider society. In understanding ESD as a form of capability, the evaluative space of education itself provides the means for significant change in how we approach the subject of business and in turn how businesses might view themselves. Crucially, the need is for more relational understanding of the broad and at times competing factors at stake in matters of sustainability. The point is not for ESD to be a necessary outcome of contemporary business, but as a forum for its radical critical thinking. This requires certain evaluative spaces and capabilities, but also in turn presents the opportunity to extend them.

1. Education for Sustainable Development: A Capability Approach

This paper offers critical reflection following the Japan Forum of Business and Society's 9th Annual Conference (2019) on the theme of Corporate Social Responsibility and Sustainability in Management Education. By way of introduction to four papers from the conference (outlined at the end of this paper) it serves to offer what is defined here as a critical, evaluative 'space' specific to Education for Sustainable Development.

This paper turns particular attention to 'Education for Sustainable Development' (ESD) in relation to business studies, which arguably expands the units of analysis to the point at which – beyond the typical purview of business – we need to question the relationship between the educational and business setting, and indeed, to question what it means to de-

liver business ethics education more fundamentally. The emergence of ESD is taken in
this paper to be a 'new disruptor' within education. This can be understood as twofold: it
represents a specific ethical agenda to assert
over existing business education, but equally
it requires a level of re-thinking about the nature of business, as to question anew how we
define business education in the first place. It
is worth noting, reference to the term 'development' in ESD is not taken here to refer to
development issues or studies per se in relation to emerging economies, but rather as a
business and educational development that is
pertinent to all economies. As outlined below
with respect to UNESCO's definition of ESD,
the critical issues are wide-ranging and interconnected globally, so pertaining to all business education contexts. As will become ap-
parent, the framing of this paper bears relation to debates between ethics and economics,
with specific reference to Amartya Sen, who
has done much to reinvigorate mainstream
economics through the contributions of moral
philosophy and welfare economics (Sen, 1987).

The significant prevalence of ESD teaching
at business schools dates to the early 2000s,
particularly following the introduction of
UNESCO's definition, which urges business
schools to accept a more comprehensive approach. While, there is no formally agreed
model, the UNESCO definition, drafted as early as 2005, usefully establishes ESD as follows:

Education for Sustainable Development
means including key sustainable development issues into teaching and learning;

for example, climate change, disaster risk
reduction, biodiversity, poverty reduction,
and sustainable consumption. It also requires participatory teaching and learning methods that motivate and empower
learners to change their behaviour and
take action for sustainable development.
Education for Sustainable Development
consequently promotes competencies like
critical thinking, imagining future scenarios and making decisions in a collaborative way[1].

The definition presents an agenda for educators and students to look at how they can
make positive changes to support sustainability through their own actions and behaviour
(Ghoshal, 2005; Rands and Starik, 2009; Starik et
al., 2010). Of particular interest for this paper
is the emphasis on an evaluative approach
and competencies for independent, critical
thinking, which raise questions about the
'means' rather than simply the 'ends' of education; and which, in turn, pose quandaries as to
how we define the parameters and intentions
of business and how best to implement and
maintain an appropriate means for the development of future leaders. Many business
schools can certainly be seen not only to
adopt the rhetoric of ESD, but also to seek to
implement its key tenets. Yet, an underlying
problem regards the status of education, as to
whether it represents a challenge to or merely the reproduction of conventional practices
(Burchell et al., 2015; Rasche and Gilbert, 2015;
Painter-Morland et al., 2016).

The account offered here chimes with the

account offered by Baden and Higgs (2015), in which they challenge the 'wisdom' of management theories and practices. They offer a critique of 'business and management school education and the values it propounds and its contribution to the development of future leaders' (p.539). Marking a distinction between means and ends, referring to 'terminal goals, such as human welfare and instrumental goals, such as money', they are explicitly critical of dominant management models that measure success purely in financial terms. 'If business is to retain its legitimacy and benefit society,'they write, 'profit needs to be seen as a means to the end of sustainable business not an end in itself' (p.539). Baden and Higgs make a laudable argument, drawing attention, for example, to the need for curriculum changes. A point echoed in this current paper is for the need to go beyond cosmetic, superficial change (as has been prevalent, for example, in presenting ethics, responsibility and sustainability through elective modules etc.), with the need 'to *integrate* relevant discussions into business schools to move beyond a situation where the topic is only treated as an add-on' (Rasche and Gilbert, 2015, p.240). However, arguing the need for change does not necessarily help in *actually* finding ways to effect change. One of the problems of Baden and Higgs' account, for example, as will be examined here, is that they are not fully reflective of the *means* through which an 'alternative' business model can be asserted.

This paper draws on the philosophical pragmatism of Amartya Sen's Capability Approach (1999). As will be argued, Sen's work enables us to ask more operative questions about how education can offer an appropriate alignment or articulation of means and ends and so providing the capability for the 'imaging of future scenarios' as hoped for in UNESCO's definition of ESD. The paper adopts Sen's (1999) underlying argument for 'development as freedom', where freedom is the principle and purpose of development. In this case, we need to consider how 'sustainability' (outlined in more detail in the next section) is to be taken as the underlying capability *of* ESD, not simply its outcome or goal. Also, it relates to debates around 'welfare economics' (propounded by Sen and others since the 1970s). We need to work towards more comprehensive accounts and perspectives, which gives rise for the need of what Sen refers to as 'evaluative space'; i.e. to understand how actions within one domain, or pertaining to specific needs, has impact on other domains and factors. If we can extend the evaluative 'space' (or the array of factors and outcomes we take into account) we can seek to reach greater consensus with businesses and wider society.

2. | SITUATING EDUCATION FOR SUSTAINABILE DEVELOPMENT

Kurucz et al. (2014, p.454) position sustainability as a 'provocation' to traditional management education, which they argue is limited in its 'capacity to address complex global issues', despite such issues being increasingly important and visible in the business world. Thus, sustainability offers a mode of critique and renewal, 'to build a new vision for management education that moves business schools beyond functioning as management training and diploma-granting facilities', and instead to 'serve as public spheres of conscientization'. It is not so much that within a curriculum that sustainability represents a defined set of learning elements within a syllabus, but that it is a *way of approaching* the subject area as a whole. Analogy can be made to learning a foreign language. The syllabus sets out a finite set of vocabulary to learn, but it also requires certain principles of grammar to be understood, which in turn enable the words to be used in a variety of ways and contexts. Ethics and sustainability can be understood more as a 'grammar' of learning. It is a way of formulating the subject and a way of maintaining and underpinning learning. As will be outlined, ESD is to be taken as a 'capability' for facilitating and enhancing further learning rather than simply as a topic of learning. Beyond the classroom, this raises searching questions about the practical and epistemological relationship between business practices, education and research, as well as more broadly the status and positioning of business practices within wider social and economic discourse.

Cullen's (2017) bibliometric review shows that since the mid-1990s the fields of business and management studies have shown a substantial growth in interest in sustainability as a general topic, and from around the mid-2000s 'the emphasis of books published in this area began to change from one which advocated "sustainable development" to one which viewed sustainability as a management practice which could help businesses and society

simultaneously' (p. 429). The specific literature within business education has been more limited, but has shown similar growth rates. Cullen notes how the rapid increase in interest, over a relatively short period of time, has led to confusions (and arguably dilutions), with a wide range of different understandings and definitions of sustainability (Marshall and Toffel, 2005; Ferdig, 2007; Parr, 2009). Equally, it can be argued interest in sustainability in mainstream business and management studies has come late, and as a result significant attention 'has yet to be integrated at any level into most business school courses and programs' (Starik et al., 2010, p. 377). By the mid-2000s, for example, while the topic was seen to have had significant take up, sustainability was nonetheless seen 'as a relative "newcomer" to the MBA curriculum' (Christensen et al., 2007, p. 352). For the purposes of this paper, sustainability is to be understood within the broad terms set out by UNESCO (outlined above), which allows for an understanding across economic, social and environmental issues. As Cullen notes, 'sustainability has been a central concern in fields such as geography, sociology and development studies for decades, [while] the relatively recent interest from management studies can be seen to stem from the various social, environmental and economic crises facing the world (2017, p. 430). As part of which, sustainability concerns both intergenerational and collaborative thinking. When UNESCO refer to 'imagining future scenarios' there is a need to understand different generational temporalities, which, in terms of short-term political cycles are not always easy to 'sustain' and make workable. Similarly, establishing and then sustaining collaboration across different domains and disciplines can prove difficult. These, then, are as much sustainability issues as are the headline concerns of finance, resources and the environment.

As will be discussed in the next section, the work of Amartya Sen is concerned with an underlying interest in the expansion of real freedoms that people can enjoy – to advance, for example, the kind of 'well-being' that Baden and Higgs suggest is the goal of education. Importantly, Sen argues for freedom as an end in itself; a 'constitutive role' of freedom, which 'relates to the importance of substantive freedom to enriching human life. The substantive freedoms include elementary capabilities like being able to avoid such deprivations as starvation, undernourishment, escapable morbidity and premature mortality', as well as freedoms of education, literacy, political participation and freedom of speech etc. (1999, p. 36). However, he also accounts for 'instrumental' freedoms and rights[2] that 'may *also* be very effective in contributing to economic progress'. These are operative in development, though still substantive freedoms remain fundamental. As Sen notes, 'the significance of the instrumental freedom of political freedom as *means* to development does not in any way reduce the evaluative importance of freedom as an *end* of development' (p. 37). An underlying tension of this paper is the degree to which issues of sustainability can be read in terms of substantive freedoms (on a par with the aforementioned elementary capabilities), or whether as more instrumental means to-

wards change. The line taken here is that in order for ESD to be instrumental to a changing landscape within business studies, so arguably impacting positively on society at large, there is equally a need to consider it more substantively – as something constitutive of how we live, or intend to live.

In discussing ESD, it is pertinent to draw attention to the 'Principles for Responsible Management Education' (PRME), since both are linked initiatives of the UN Global Compact. At its core, PRME is directed at the next generation of business professionals. As Parkes et al., (2017) outline:

> ...the underlying goal [in establishing PRME] was to develop the capabilities of our students to be generators of sustainable value for a more inclusive global economy through our teaching, research, and campus practices. Then UN Secretary-General Ban Ki-Moon, pointing to the potential of the PRME initiative, noted that, "The Principles for Responsible Management Education have the capacity to take the case for universal values and business into classrooms on every continent" (p. 61)

The Secretary-General's words undoubtedly suggest of a more inclusive, interconnected set of relationships. It is interesting how we might read the phrase 'universal values and business', whether we take the 'and' as an operator between two entities, or as a means to intrinsically link the two. Parkes et al.'s (2017) reference to students as 'generators' and in having 'capabilities' in the first instance would seem to suggest of a working *out from* business, so to impact upon the wider world. Yet, over time, this may lead to a different conception of where the boundaries lie, if indeed they need to exist at all between business and society[3].

Currently, if we look at the 'Eligibility Procedures and Accreditation Standards for Business Accreditation' of the well-known AACSB International (The Association to Advance Collegiate Schools of Business), it is evident that, while the overall vision is for business and business schools to be 'a force for good, contributing to the world's economy and to society', the thrust of the language emphases business as somehow separate to (even if 'serving') society or communities. It uses phrases such as: 'society is increasingly demanding that companies become more accountable', 'the same factors impacting business also are changing higher education', and 'business schools must respond to the business world's changing needs by providing relevant knowledge and skills to the communities they serve'. Of course the purpose of such a body is to set accreditation standards, which inevitably leads it to narrow its focus, in this case business education (and so the site of business practices more generally). Yet, the accreditation bodies are arguably themselves looking to innovate and to be more responsive to the colleges they interact with. As AACSB International's documentation puts it: 'Accreditation standards and associated processes should foster quality and consistency, but not at the expense of the creativity and experimentation

necessary for innovation. Also, accreditation standards and processes should not impede experimentation or entrepreneurial pursuits; the standards must recognize that innovation involves both the potential for success and the risk of failure' (AACSB, 2017, p. 3)[4]. There is a need to look beyond prescriptions and instead consider underlying capabilities and how these can align with aspirations.

Various stakeholders are all looking in the same direction, towards a more progressive business landscape. What is missing, however, is a cohesive means of proceeding. It is in this respect that Sen's perspective of a 'Capability Approach' can be useful to redefine problems as questions around the appropriate capabilities required to achieve certain functions. As a long-time advocate of welfare economics, involving the co-consideration of ethics and economics (Sen, 1987; Putnam, 2004, pp. 46–64), for Sen there is a need to re-evaluate the way we relate to debates of the market; i.e. how we position ourselves vis-à-vis business *and* society. The most prominent argument in favour of the market mechanism is that left unrestricted it typically allows income and wealth to flow (and 'trickle down'), which broadly Sen agrees to, with some caveats. However, his argument for the market is different, and more fundamental, regarding an inalienable right to undertake exchange and transactions. 'Even if such rights are not accepted as being inviolable,' he writes, '...it can still be argued that there is some social loss involved in denying people the right to interact economically with each other' (1999, p. 26). Added to which, he notes, '[t] he discipline of economics has tend-ed to move away from focusing on the value of freedom to that of utilities, incomes and wealth. The narrowing of focus leads to an underappreciation of the full role of the market mechanism' (p. 27). In Sen's view, then, there is a need to rebalance the 'engineered' or highly mathematical approach to twentieth century economics, through the reintroduction of ethics (Putnam, 2004, pp. 47-48). It is worth noting, in Sen's case, 'the reintroduction of ethical concerns and concepts into economic discourse must not be thought of as an *abandonment* of "classical economics"; rather it is the *reintroduction* of something that was everywhere present in the writings of Adam Smith' (Putnam, 2004, p. 48). Sen aligns strongly with the work of Adam Smith. He notes wryly how commentators often rarely get beyond the famous quote of 'the benevolence of the butcher, the brewer, or the baker', but suggests, even if they do not read further, 'this passage would indicate that what Smith is doing here is to specify why and how normal transactions in the market are carried out', and that crucially, 'the fact that Smith noted that mutually advantageous trades are very common does not indicate at all that he thought that self-love ⋯ could be adequate for a good society. Indeed, he maintained precisely the opposite. He did not rest economic salvation on some unique motivation' (Sen, 1987, pp. 23-24). Thus, Sen reminds of the underlying *social* principle of economics. We always trade with others. It is a freedom we seek to secure, which can only be secured *through* the relations with others, rather than despite them. In effect, exchange comes *before*

business, it is one of the fundaments of being social. In this view, we can begin to view any rigid distinction between business *and* society as problematic.

As will be considered further below, Sen's focus on capabilities and 'freedoms' *as* development (not the result of development), sets out a more pragmatic and interconnected understanding of the market, wealth and sociality, which we can adopt to make better sense of how ESD needs to be conceptualised and articulated within the context of the business school. While Sen certainly does not dismiss classical economics, his reading, as suggested above, is nuanced and reintroduces philosophical and ethical considerations relevant to contemporary debates. By making a link, then, ESD represents one opportunity to rethink how we define the curriculum for a new generation. What needs to take effect is not only a framework (and set of accreditation standards) for articulating new values[5], but also a *means* allowing for 'the next generation of managers, leaders, and business professionals, committed to developing their capabilities to be generators of sustainable value for a more inclusive global economy' (Parkes et al., 2017, p. 62). It is in this direction that Sen's 'Capability Approach' offers valuable insights.

3. │ COMPREHENSIVE OUTCOMES

The agenda of ESD in itself puts forward a need for change – to change the curriculum, to change behaviours, to change business practices. Institutionally, this gives educators and administrators a 'case for change', but as already intimated, implementation of new approaches can end up being superficial, or at least bolted on rather than built in. In other words ESD is readily *incorporated* into the educational programme, but it is not necessarily constitutive of it. At stake is a wider range of capabilities for a transformative understanding of business. Underlying Sen's work is the need for an integrated picture. He notes, for example, how various economic indicators in isolation can be used to show disparities in wealth between countries, but when combined with other factors such as health statistics produce quite striking and unexpected disparities. For example, male survival rates in the USA are higher than that of the state of Kerala, India, by over a decade. The obvious explanation is that the USA is vastly more affluent and so people live longer. Yet, the same statistics show that black males living in USA have a *lower* survival rate than in Kerala. What Sen argues with these statistics is the importance of *combined* factors, or 'substantive freedoms' as he calls them. These include aspects of social and health care, community relations, education, law and order, security, and political factors (notably the level of democracy). In order to attend to issues such as poverty and health it is not enough to simply spend more money. Businesses, for example, can often be criticised for the ineffectiveness of philanthropic activity; for only donating to, not actually *contributing* to society. Development is not merely a return on investment and it is not a luxury: '...enhancement of human freedom is both the main object and the primary means of development. The ob-

jective of development relates to the valuation of the actual freedoms enjoyed by the people involved. Individual capabilities crucially depend on, among other things, economic, social, and political arrangements' (Sen, 1999, p. 53).

Sen's account of 'development as freedom' might be described best as the *freedom to* do things (to live according to your own capabilities), rather than suggest of the more negative *freedom from* something. In other words, development is not applied to free us from a problem, instead it is the articulation of our freedom. According to Sen's data, males living in Kerala will on average earn substantially less than black males living in the USA, but potentially possess more *substantive* freedoms (in terms of education, social networks, literary etc.). And it is these substantive freedoms that he argues *combine* to lead to longer life expectancy. Crucially, a combined ethics and economic perspective looks to the bigger picture, so asking different questions of and across datasets. Similarly, ESD requires a broader canvas to be taken into account, which itself is challenging of the field of business studies.

The factors involved in ESD are of course different to those pertaining specifically to poverty, well-being and life expectancy, but similar principles are at stake (and there are interrelated debates). Firstly, ESD should not be viewed as development on from traditional business, or indeed as an imposition upon, or even policing of, existing business practices. This would be to suggest ESD is somehow seeking *freedom from* business (forever characterised as bad). Alternatively, the view might be taken that business and commerce has matured to a point at which it is now possible to apply ESD. Again, this would be the wrong way to frame things, as if ESD is a luxury we can now afford. The point is to consider ESD as the *freedom to* pursue business in a particular way, one which offers a more integrated picture and so is both led by and leads to greater capability. As Sen writes: 'Capability is thus a kind of freedom: the substantive freedom to achieve alternative functioning combinations (or, less formally put, the freedom to achieve various lifestyles)' (1999, p.75). The use of the term 'functioning' varies across Sen's work, but as Hart (2013, pp.37–38) notes, the term generally gravitates to 'achieved functionings', made possible through an individual's 'capability set'. As Sen writes: 'The capability set would consist of the alternative functioning vectors … While the combination of a person's functionings reflects her actual *achievements*, the capability set reflects the *freedom* to achieve: the alternative functioning combinations from which this person can choose' (1999, p.75). Sen gives the example of how an affluent person choosing to fast has a very different 'capability set' (or set of choices) than the destitute person unable to feed themselves[6].

Given the various (and even competing) demands and perspectives encapsulated by ESD, we can think of it as an attempt to bring together a variety of 'lifestyles' or choices, which represents a complex 'capability set', all of which needs attention and evaluation. Following this logic, it is necessary to consider what substantive freedoms are required of business within the frame of ESD.

Education itself is one key freedom or capability. We need the ability to think critically and creatively in order to re-evaluate and transform business. Thus, the capabilities of a teacher to deliver the kind of education they value is important in itself, but equally this is part of the greater freedom to understand sustainable development, and for education to provide support to business thinking, to allow for a wider set of viewpoints. In this sense, education is not simply about feeding business with appropriately skilled labour to enable the status quo. Education is to be taken as a substantive freedom of business itself. It is part of an infrastructure that gives individuals and individual businesses the means to pursue the values they deem to be important. From Sen's perspective, intervention is not what makes changes, but only what supports it. What we require are the grounds for change, which form the freedom to assert change. It can be argued that economic development can better support and resource education, yet Sen (1999, p.41) sees this the other way round, arguing education is a freedom supportive of economic development. Education is for example capability towards the function of greater productivity. He cites, for example, the East Asian economic 'miracle' as being strongly predicated on 'human resource development' and higher levels of literacy, underlying which – in this particular context and circumstance – is a common cultural and social investment in the primacy of education. With respect to ESD, education is not simply a driver towards greater productivity, but towards *better* (and sustainable) business practices.

Capability Approach pays attention not only to opportunities but also processesor procedures 'that allow freedom of actions and decisions' (Sen, 1999, p.17). The idea of understanding 'development as freedom' leads us to pose different kinds of questions about what we think development means, and how it correlates to ideas of freedom. In effect, Sen turns our frames of reference around, to understand freedom not as the 'goal' (whether development, or education), so not as an *end*, but equally as *means*. This is given further definition through his distinction between 'culmination outcomes' and 'comprehensive outcomes'. Taking a hypothetical idea that a competitive market mechanism could be matched by a centralized, even dictatorial system, Sen asks – if both yield the same economic result – is there any real difference if we concern ourselves only with end results? Intuitively, he writes, 'something would be missing in such a scenario ... the freedom of people to act as they like in deciding on where to work, what to produce, what to consume and so on' (Sen, 1999, p.27). Despite being able to produce the same end results, the argument is that we would still prefer the scenario offering free choice. The difference is between whether or not we focus on just the ends, or equally upon the means; and that such means are constitutive of the ends, i.e. it is how we define ourselves through the process as much as the end[7].

Sen's explicit interest in capabilities is of more specific import, providing a pragmatic way of analysing a situation and of defining development or change *through capabilities*. It can be viewed a form of idealism, Sen refers to 'outcomes' (and is context specific). His approach, in looking at the processes and procedures that allow for opportunities, as a *combined reading*, and which vary enormously between different situations, is concerned with development as a *form* of action and doing, not simply a value or belief (which arguably can remain merely an ideological pronouncement).

Thus, for Sen, there is a distinction 'between "culmination outcomes" (that is, only final outcomes without taking any note of the process of getting there, including the exercise of freedom) and "comprehensive outcomes" (taking note of the processes through which the culmination outcomes come about)'. The relative merits of a market system, he argues, is not based solely on the 'capacity to generate more efficient culmination outcomes' (1999, p.27). In the context of ESD, there are numerous different ways for its implementation within the education setting, which in turn can be reflected in simple measures and accreditations. However, if we look to how implementation *culminates*, i.e. how ESD is 'actually existing' and how it progresses beyond the educational context, we might come to quite different views about how best to pursue it. In an ever increasingly regulated society, with numerous systems of accreditation and auditing, universities and companies have become skilful in appropriately positioning their activities (and without necessarily making fundamental changes to their practices). In this sense the implementing and integrating of ESD (as a culmination outcome) is not necessarily the same as its embedding (Rasche and Gilbert, 2015). For that, we need to understand – as active forces – the integrated context of education, business and society. ESD provides a prompt to redraft how we define these terms, and indeed how these sites of practice interrelate, so allowing for the imaging of future scenarios, as UNESCO would hope for, and for a broader 'evaluative space' (to adopt Sen's term, explored further below), whereby a wider range of options and interactions can be taken into critical consideration.

4. | EVALUATIVE SPACE: ESD AS CAPABILITY

If we review the various issues that UNESCO list in their definition of ESD, such as climate change, biodiversity, poverty, and sustainable consumption, and others such beside, each in turn are laudable concerns. However, difficulties may arise if we start to consider them in relation to one another. For example, is there a hierarchy of low to high priority, and in attending to one issue can we remain true to others? Overcoming issues of poverty could in some circumstances lead to increased production, or a decrease in biodiversity (where perhaps greenbelt land is used to overcome housing shortages etc.). Wilkinson and Pickett (2010) argue that improvements to quality of life and equality can be met without further economic growth. Indeed, their thesis is that equality and sustainability are intrinsically linked. Sen's Capability Approach is attuned to these kinds of interrelated concerns. In discussing equality, for example, he is critical of a utili-

tarian perspective, which puts 'equal weights on everyone's utility gains' (1992, p. 13), when in fact, he argues, we cannot assume all individuals can achieve the same utility gain from the same resources or circumstances. Thus, despite general agreement that equality is a good thing, it is not something we can necessarily uniformly agree upon in practice. As much as we may need to debate the importance of equality, for Sen, the question is also always 'equality of what?' (Sen, 1992). Being egalitarian, he argues 'is not a "uniting" feature'. Indeed, he writes, 'it is precisely because there are such substantive differences between the endorsement of different spaces in which equality is recommended ... that the basic similarity between them (in the form of wanting equality is *some* space that is seen as important) can be far from transparent' (1992, p. 14). Similarly, the question of 'why sustainability?' can appear to dominate, whereas, *pace* Sen, we should really ask 'sustainability of what?'. The answer to which will vary depending on numerous factors. And like equality, there are some 'spaces' of sustainability (as Sen terms it) that are more readily associated than others. So, for example, the environment can quickly be evoked, yet, as noted in this essay, the issues range more broadly. The protest movement, #BlackLivesMatter, for example, has sought to show how environmental concerns such as air pollution are also deeply entwined with matters of class and race (Kelbert, 2016)[8]. What Sen has to say of equality can be transposed to matters of sustainability: 'it is important to recognize equality in one space – no matter how hallowed by tradition – can lead one to be anti-egalitarian in some other space, the comparative importance of which in the overall assessment has to be critically assessed' (1992, p. 16).

The frequent reference to 'space' needs some clarification. The Capability Approach is concerned with what Sen refers to as 'evaluative space', which is never definitively defined, certainly not as a specific site or domain. Nonetheless, looking across his writings, we can relate 'space' to a form of operation that varies according to different domains, discourses and disciplines. Different professional, conceptual and discursive domains or spaces will emphasise different 'objects of value':

> The identification of the objects of value specifies what may be called an *evaluative space*. In standard utilitarian analysis, for example, the evaluative space consists of the individual utilities (defined in the usual terms of pleasures, happiness, or desire fulfilment). [...] The capability approach is concerned primarily with your identification of value-objects, and sees the evaluative space in terms of functioning and capabilities to function (Sen, 1993, p. 32).

As already discussed, capability sets provide possibility of different choices or functions. All of which, however, sit within 'spaces' (meaning domains or discourses), which are inevitably important in driving the terms of debate. Different evaluative spaces or agendas will have a strong impact on how we come to view capabilities and functionings in the first place. To quote Sen at length:

The selection of the evaluative space has a good deal of cutting power on its own, both because of what it *includes* as potentially valuable and because of what it *excludes*. For example, because of the nature of the evaluative space, the capability approach differs from utilitarian evaluation ... in making room for a variety of human acts and states as important in themselves (not just *because* they may produce utility, nor just to the *extent* that they yield utility). It also makes room for valuing various freedoms – in the form of capabilities. On the other side, the approach does not attach direct – as opposed to derivative – importance to the *means* of living or *means* of freedom (e.g. real income, wealth, opulence, primary goods, or resources), as some other approaches do. These variables are not part of the evaluative space, though they can indirectly influence the evaluation through their effects on variables included in that space (Sen, 1993, p. 33).

Education provides an obvious context in which not only can we engage with an evaluative space, but also potentially to construct one. ESD in particular presents specific means to pursue the relational complexity that is suggestive of Sen's account. However, as discussed above, the implementation of ESD and the pressures of various drivers can inhibit how we frame or engage in the issues. Baden and Higgs (2015), as shown, are critical of the dominant approaches, suggesting that 'ethical issues tend to be presented as instrumental rather than the infusion of wisdom into the curriculum' (p.545). Nonetheless, they outline a number of areas where a wider frame of reference and perspective can be adopted to broaden the purview of business studies. So, for example, they suggest Accounting modules can work upon the concept of the triple bottom line (Elkington, 1997), to broaden out from economic to social and environmental performance. Finance, while potentially more difficult, can look at financing that contributes positively to social needs. Human resource management can turn to 'quality of life' indices to offer justifications for improved working conditions not on the basis of improved productivity, but on the human value. Marketing is another difficult area, as arguably it is predicated on consumption, which then is in tension with sustainability issues. Nonetheless, it is possible to promote decreases in production and focus on shifts to services. Entrepreneurialism can be centred around inspirational prosocial role models, and corporate governance modules can look to alternative legal models and structures, and strategy modules can emphasize stakeholders over shareholders (Baden and Higgs, 2015, pp.546–548).

Each of these examples suggest changes to what might be *included* or *excluded* in the 'space' of the curriculum and teaching environment. Of course, a key concern is the *extent* to which such changes are made. They can be presented as mere alternative functionings, so becoming just one choice out of a range of choices. As such, a compartmental-

ised approach is still followed. We might even relate this to a more utilitarian mode, as a means to *maximise* sustainability in a given area, without necessarily broaching its deeper significance. Certainly, it is the case, through modularisation, that the different subject areas may not necessarily interact. Samuelson notes, for example, 'a course with "sustainability" in the title might consider the risks for both the business and its fence-line neighbors, ... But in finance and other classes, these same students are taught to externalize costs and discount the future' (p.67). However, if we are to see ESD as genuinely broadening a capability set, and evoking a different kind of evaluative space, it is important to maintain a critical dialogue between differing perspectives and needs. As Cebrián, Grace & Humphris (2013, p.286) put it, 'ESD can foster a sustainable social transformation, through the clarification and reassessment of values;' indeed 'sustainability can be defined as a learning process that encourages transformative learning, the capacity to challenge existing patterns and worldviews, to construct new knowledge collectively, to rethink current practice, and to critique and examine sustainability issues' (p.287); an argument that echoes Kurucz et al. (2014).

The evaluative space determines key considerations or the terms of debate, even the degree to which sustainability might be viewed as significant in the first place. Education can clearly play a role in influencing and even re-calibrating such spaces. However, within such a context is it also how we relate to capabilities that is important. 'The freedom to lead different types of life,' writes Sen, 'is reflected in the person's capability set' (1993, p.33). This is by no means an unproblematic notion. We might not always be aware of our capabilities, or we may not always have impetus to make choices despite being available to us. Furthermore compound issues, such as mentioned above in relation to environment and race, are either not easily visible, or can become so entrenched that limited capability is normalised. To give an example specific to sustainability and the business context, we might consider the differing capability sets of a large, nationwide car dealership and a small, local mechanics firm. With the former, narratives pertinent to sustainability can often be made quite explicit. Perhaps the company promotes a new line in hybrid or electric cars, and/or a scrappage scheme framed explicitly as a 'green' service. A problem, of course, is that the business is also predicated on increasing sales, so adding to the number of cars on the road. It is focused on providing new cars, rather than new components. Down the road, the local mechanic does not necessarily see him- or herself as being particularly diligent towards issues of sustainability, yet as a business the focus is on repairing cars, keeping them on the road. It is about re-using resources. These businesses engage differently with the evaluative space concerning sustainability. One is overt about such evaluations. Indeed, the car dealership is likely to have a dedicated CSR report and provide lots of related signage on its premises to impress its customers. Such displays of 'consciousness' on the part of the business could be said to further influence future capabilities. However, what is significant about Sen's work is the need to *relate between* different circumstances and indicators – to understand relational differences and that change occurs *through* circumstances. In this case, while the mechanic is perhaps not so consciously engaged in the evaluative space of sustainability issues, it does not mean the business is not already in possession of requisite capabilities and indeed already functioning in a sustainable way. The question over 'sustainability of what?' is again pertinent. As Sen argues, capability is not a resource of fixed value, but something that must be examined in terms of its scaling according to specific circumstances. The difficulty, of course, is bringing legitimacy and/or consciousness to such capabilities. At this level, as Putnam (2004, p.60) reminds, census around matters of capability requires public debate and democratic engagement and acceptance. In this case, the car dealership perhaps speaks more publicly, yet in looking to a new generation of business practitioners a wider, relational field of vision allows us to look more across different capabilities, to make finer judgements about what is valuable. Again, it is arguably the educational 'space' that has a vital role to play.

Inevitably, there are various critiques and challenges made of Sen's work (Hart, 2013, pp.34–46; Qizilbash, M., 1996; 2008; Gasper, 2002; Clark, 2005; Cohen, 1993). It is not in the scope of this paper to work through these in detail, but in closing a few points can be made. Sen is criticised for a lack of clarity in the use of his terms (which have evolved over his career).

This paper has sought to clarify the key concepts as far as possible within the narrative provided here. As Hart (2013, p. 35) notes, there are many terms, such as class, power and poverty, that are equally difficult to define, but their contested nature is equally constitutive of our need to debate the issues that surround them. This is the case too of 'sustainability', which, as argued in terms of ESD, should *not* be fixed, but always the subject of debate. 'Freedom' is another term of significant complexity and is central to Sen's work. Qizilbash (1996) has been critical of a lack of attention to 'negative freedom', i.e. the forces to take us away from freedom. Sen could be seen as overly optimistic. However, rather like the debates around the concept of the 'public sphere', which is really only something of an ideal, even a myth, most critics hold the view that it is a 'necessary possibility', as something we must work towards even if not always reached. Likewise, 'capability' may not necessarily be something we can distinctively identify or agree upon, but it becomes an important concept through which we can make empirical judgements about how best to approach topics such as 'sustainability' (within the specific space, for example, of business and business education). As part of which, the argument made here to keep debate open, to continually test circumstances etc., echoes Sen's reluctance to offer specific 'lists' of capabilities and functions. By contrast, Nussbaum, an associate of Sen and an important scholar of capability theory in her own right, has been more forthright about the need to develop schema. An implication for future research,

when looking at ESD through the lens of capability approach, would be whether or not Nussbaum's (2003) consideration of 'fundamental entitlements' and 'minimum thresholds' might in fact be pertinent to establishing aspects of curriculum and its tie-up with business practices. Finally, a key criticism of Sen's work is in 'under-emphasizing the role of social interaction in the generation of capabilities' (Hart, 2013, p. 44). This, again, is an area that requires further research. The approach taken in this paper is that the conceptual approach – to understand specific principles of means and ends, to privilege comprehensive outcomes, and to give credence to *sets* of capability etc. – is something that translates when we consider 'individual' sites of practice, such as a firm or the interaction of businesses. Also, in terms of ESD, specifically (i.e. in the context of education), the ideas of capability do generally apply, even if more theorisation is welcomed (Hart, 2013, pp. 45–46). Overall, ESD is a critical prompt for the expansion of the evaluative space of business, which needs to be addressed through a broadening of capabilities both within and outside of the educational setting itself.

5. | TOWARDS A NEW DIALOGUE

This paper has examined the emergence of Education for Sustainable Development (ESD) within the field of business and management studies. The body of current literatures tend to focus on the development of teaching ethics and sustainability in a compartmentalised way, with less attention on how business can engage dynamically with such a new agenda (i.e. the wider ramifications its inscribes). To support a *change* in agenda, consideration has been made of Sen's Capability Approach, which leads to the view that ESD itself can be understood a form of capability. In the context of education it is an evaluative space that provides the means for significant change in how we approach the subject of business and in turn how businesses might view themselves. Crucially, the need is for more relational understanding of the broad and at times competing factors and agents at stake in matters of sustainability. Current practices in implementing and accrediting ESD can lead to a de-coupling from the actual educational practices of a business school. Such decoupling may be caused where ESD is seen as an end point of strategic renewal, not as a means of educating, expanding on and practicing in relation to ethics and sustainability issues. Sen's formulation of 'development as freedom', by which he means we need freedom or capability to be able to pursue development (i.e., freedom is not a product of development, but its means), is significant in turning the tables in how we relate to the issues of ESD. We might argue, not for *sustainability as ESD* (i.e. that ESD can lead to sustainability), but rather *ESD as sustainability*, that sustainable thinking and actions, or capability are *required* for ESD to take root. The point is not for ESD to be some form of 'necessary' outcome, but as a genuine practice based on an expanded 'evaluative space', allowing for *comprehensive* outcomes. Of course, one of the real difficulties of ESD is the radical critical thinking it implies,

which leads to a challenging of received knowledge and norms. Nonetheless, not only does this critical work require certain evaluative spaces and capabilities, it also in turn presents the opportunity to extend them.

Overall, then, the account offered here has sought to provide the critical, conceptual tool of 'evaluative space' in relation to ESD. It is offered as a contribution to the Japan Forum of Business and Society's 9th Annual Conference 2019, which was held around the themes of Corporate Social Responsibility and Sustainability in Management Education. Specifically, the paper seeks to aid an understanding of forward-going, progressive engagements with ESD, and in particular serves to offer critical dialogue with four papers from the conference: Elisabeth Fröhlich and Berivan Kul's 'The Necessity of Sustainability in Management Education'; Masao Seki's 'サステナブルビジネス教育における課題：トランスフォーメーションの時代に求められるもの' [Challenges in Sustainable Business Education −What is Required in the Age of Transformation]; Yasushi Sonobe and Makiko Kawakita's 'The Prestige Effects of Sponsorship on Attitudes toward Corporate Brands and Art Events'; and Hidemitsu Sasaya's 'SDGs を活用した新たな共通価値の創造 (CSV)' [Evolution of Creating Shared Value (CSV) by Utilizing SDGs]. The first of these two papers illustrate how educators and professionals in their own evaluative space consider approaches to, and engage in, the practice of ESD. The other two papers present investigations that offer contexts exemplifying 'objects of value' and lead towards a question of 'what' is to be located among consumers, organisations and society.

The paper by Fröhlich and Kultake on the task by discussing a case from the CBS International Business School, to explain its sustainability vision in terms of serving as a role model for other business schools. They argue that 'Rethinking Capitalism' is one of the essential requirements to respond to ecological and social challenges we face today. It is a particular interest of this paper to consider how a business school approaches its curriculum design comprehensively in order to contribute to achieving the Sustainable Development Goals (SDGs). They propose 'SDG teaching mapping' as the means of engaging in this process. As an example of this mapping exercise, SDG12's targets are utilized to evaluate current practices and so to identify opportunities and directions in terms of curriculum design in the future. The paper by Seki argues that achieving SDGs requires not only progressive improvement but transformation that would make major social and economic changes at the system level (e.g., one of the keys is digital transformation). He points out that companies are the driving force behind such transformation and places importance on 'future aspiration', 'strategic thinking' and 'backcasting' while nurturing people who can create innovation. Backcasting refers to identifying what needs to be done now as a plan, after defining what would be a desirable state in the future. The paper certainly triggers key questions regarding what we value: *what and where* do 'we' want to be in the future? Indeed, ultimately, to ask: *what is a good life*?

The paper by Sonobe and Kawakita presents an investigation on the relationship between corporate prestige and corporate image by supporting artistic activities. In particular, it examines the effects of prestige in sponsorships on consumers' attitudes toward corporate brands and art events. While reading, one may ask whether *doing* 'good' actually equates to *being* 'good'. The paper provides context to deepen our understanding of how we evaluate corporations every day: Does it matter, for example, who the 'good doers' are (e.g. corporations) and who (e.g. consumers) evaluates them? The paper by Sasaya, which similarly notes that addressing social issues has become an important business proposition for many corporations, develops a reading of the notion of Creating Shared Value (Porter and Kramer, 2011). However, he finds it problematic that there has been insufficient insight into the social issues to be addressed. He argues SDGs help articulate social issues and proposes they complement a process of creating new, shared values.

(1)　http://www.unesco.org/new/en/unesco-world-conference-on-esd-2014/resources/what-is-esd/. Accessed June 3rd 2020.

(2)　Sen (1999, pp. 36-40) identifies five types of instrumental reason: (1) political freedoms, (2) economic facilities, (3) social opportunities, (4) transparency guarantees and (5) protective securities. These freedoms 'contribute to the general capability of a person to live more freely, but they also serve to complement one another', thus analysis 'must also take note of the empirical linkages that tie the distinct types of freedom *together*, strengthening their joint importance' (38). As an example, he notes that a rich person prevented from speaking openly is *deprived* of their freedom. 'Development seen as enhancement of freedom cannot but address such deprivations' (37).

(3)　It is worth noting conceptions of and relations between business and society can be seen to differ culturally. Tange (2001), for example, presents a contrast between Anglo-American and Japanese models of community, whereby the former places individuals and companies as separate entities within society (as the overarching community), whereas in the latter, individuals are placed within companies, which in turn provides community. The fact that the relationship between business and society is not fixed, but changeable, is pertinent to the agenda of ESD that look towards making more radical change.

(4)　AACSB Business Accreditation Standards http://www.aacsb.edu/-/media/aacsb/docs/accreditation/standards/business-2017-update.ashx?la=en, Accessed October 21st 2017.

(5)　It is important to note, the Global Compact itself can be criticised for favouring business (Thérien and Pouliot, 2006) and enabling firms to promote themselves ethically regardless of actual practices and commitments (Sethi and Schepers, 2014).

(6)　Sen's use of the terms 'capability set' and 'functioning vectors', stems from *Commodities and Capabilities* (1985). Based on a series of lectures, this is an overtly econometric text, full of equations etc., unlike his more well-known and accessible text, *Development as Freedom* (1999). It is the earlier text that helps make more sense of these terms as mathematical concepts. Capability refers to an array or set of data, which define possibilities or choices (not so distant from the concept of opportunity cost as calculable values). While functioning refers to treatments that can be drawn out from these sets (hence functioning vectors). Choices can be made based on certain principles or needs. For example, choices from a set that allow for education can be made a function. However, it is only the availability of a set that can allow for functionings in the first place.

(7)　It would be possible to explore further a view on 'means' and 'end' in Baden and Higgs' work (2015) whose view is similar to Sen. However, it is not done so due to the limited space of this paper.

(8)　Sen (1992, p. 55) similarly identifies, '[t]he problem of entrenched deprivation is particularly serious in many cases of inequality. It applies particu-

larly to the differentiation of class, community, caste, and gender'. And the extent of such deprivations can often not show up as a metric simply because individuals come to accept hardships; 'the victims do not go on grieving and lamenting all the time, and very often make great efforts to take pleasure in small mercies...'.

〈References〉

Baden, D. and Higgs, M. (2015) 'Challenging the perceived wisdom of management theories and practice', *Academy of Management Learning & Education*, Volume 14, No. 4, pp. 539-555.

Burchell, J., Murray, A. and Kennedy, S. (2015) 'Responsible management education in UK business schools: Critically examining the role of the United Nations Principles for Responsible Management Education as a driver for change', *Management Learning*, Volume 46, Issue 4, pp. 479-497.

Cebrián, G., Grace, M. and Humphris, D. (2013) 'Organisational learning towards sustainability in higher education', *Sustainability Accounting, Management and Policy Journal*, Volume 4, Issue 3, pp. 285-306.

Christensen, L.J., Peirce, E., Hartman, L.P., Hoffman, W.M. and Carrier, J. (2007) 'Ethics, CSR, and sustainability education in the Financial Times top 50 global business schools: Baseline data and future research directions', *Journal of Business Ethics*, Volume 73, Issue 4, pp. 347-368.

Clark, D.A. (2005) 'The capability approach: Its development, critiques and recent advances', *Global Poverty Research Group*, Available at http://www.gprg.org/pubs/workingpapers/pdfs/gprg-wps-032.pdf, Accessed October 21st 2017.

Cohen, G.A. (1993) 'Equality of what? On welfare, goods, and capabilities', In M. C. Nussbaum and A. Sen (Eds) *The Quality of Life* (pp. 9-29). Clarendon, Oxford.

Cullen, J.G. (2017) 'Educating Business Students About Sustainability: A Bibliometric Review of Current Trends and Research Needs', *Journal of Business Ethics*, Volume 145, Issue 2, pp. 429-439.

Elkington, J. (1997) *Cannibals with forks, The triple bottom line of 21st century business*, Oxford: Capstone Publishing Ltd.

Ferdig, M.A. (2007) 'Sustainability leadership: Co-creating a sustainable future', *Journal of Change Management*, Volume 7, No. 1, pp. 25-35.

Gasper, D. (2002) 'Is Sen's capability approach an adequate basis for considering human development?', *Review of Political Economy*, Volume 14, No. 4, pp. 435-461.

Ghoshal, S. (2005) 'Bad management theories are destroying good management practices', *Academy of Management Learning and Education*, Volume 4, No. 1, pp. 75-91.

Hart, C.S. (2013) *Aspirations, Education and Social Justice: Applying Sen and Bourdieu*, Bloomsbury, London.

Kelbert, A.W. (2016) 'Climate change is a racist crisis: that's why Black Lives Matter closed an airport', *The Guardian*, Available at https://www.theguardian.com/commentisfree/2016/sep/06/climate-change-racist-crisis-london-city-airport-black-lives-matter, Accessed October 17th 2017.

Kurucz, E.C., Colbert, B.A. and Marcus, J. (2014) 'Sustainability as a provocation to rethink management education: Building a progressive educative practice', *Management Learning*, Volume 45, Issue 4, pp. 437-457.

Marshall, J. D. and Toffel, M. W. (2005) Framing the elusive concept of sustainability: A sustainability hierarchy, *Environmental Science and Technology*, 39 (3), 673-682.

Nussbaum, M.C. (2003) 'Capabilities as Fundamental Entitlements: Sen and Social Justice', *Feminist Economics*, Volume 9, No. 2-3, pp. 33-59.

Painter-Morland, M., Sabet, E., Molthan-Hill, P., Goworek, H. and de Leeuw, S. (2016) 'Beyond the curriculum: Integrating sustainability into business schools', *Journal of Business Ethics*, Volume 139, pp. 737-754.

Parr, A. (2009) *Hijacking sustainability*, MIT Press, Cambridge MA.

Parkes, C., Buono, A.F. and Howaidy, G. (2017) 'The principles of responsible management education (PRME): The first decade – What has been achieved? The next decade – Responsible management education's challenge for the sustainable development goals (SDGs)', *The International Journal of Management Education*, Volume 15, Issue 2, Part B, pp. 61-65.

Porter, M.E. and Kramer, M.R. (2011) Creating Shared Value, *Harvard Business Review*, Vol. 89 (January-February), pp. 62-77.

Putnam, H. (2004) *The Collapse of the Fact/Value Dichotomy, and Other Essays*, Harvard University Press, Cambridge, Mass.

Qizilbash, M. (1996) 'Capabilities, well-being and human development: A survey', *Journal of Development Studies*, Volume 33, No. 2, pp. 143-162.

—— (2008) 'Amartya Sen's capability view: Insightful sketch or distorted picture?' In F. Comim, M. Qizilbash, and S. Alkire (Eds.) *The Capability Approach. Concepts, Measures and Applications* (pp. 53-81), Cambridge University Press, Cambridge.

Rands, G.P. and Starik, M. (2009) 'The short and glorious history of sustainability in North American management education', In C. Wankel & J.A.F. Stoner (Eds.) *Management Education for Global Sustainability* (pp. 19-50), IAP, New York.

Rasche, A. and Gilbert, D.U. (2015) 'Decoupling responsible management education: Why business schools may not walk their talk', *Journal of Management Inquiry*, Volume 24, Issue 3, pp. 239-252.

Samuelson, J.F. (2013) Putting Pinstripes in Persptive, *BizEd*, May/June, pp. 66-67.

Sen, A. (1985) *Commodities and Capabilities*, North-Holland, Amsterdam.

—— (1987) *On Ethics and Economics*, Basil Blackwell, Oxford.

—— (1992) *Inequality Reexamined*, Clarendon Press, Oxford.

—— (1993) 'Capability and Well-Being', In M. Nussbaum and A. Sen (eds.) *The Quality of Life* (pp. 30-53), Clarendon, Oxford.

—— (1999) *Development as Freedom*, Alfred A., Knopf, New York.

Sethi, S. P. and Schepers, D. H. (2014) United Nations Global Compact: The Promise–Performance Gap, *Journal of Business Ethics*, 122: 193-208.

Starik, M., Rands, G., Marcus, A.A. and Clark, T.S. (2010) 'From the guest editors: In search of sustainability in management education', *Academy of Management Learning and Education*, Volume 9, Issue 3, pp. 377-383.

Tange, H. (2001) *A Study on the Social Nature of Corporate Management* [Kigyo Keiei no Syakaisei Kenkyu], Chuo Keizai Sha, Tokyo.

Thérien, J.-P. and Pouliot, V. (2006) The Global Compact: Shifting the Politics of International Development?, *Global Governance: A Review of Multilateralism and International Organizations*, 12 (1), 55-76.

Wilkinson, R. and Pickett, K. (2010) *The Spirit Level: Why Equality is Better for Everyone*, Penguin, London.

The Necessity of Sustainability in Management Education

Elisabeth Fröhlich

President, CBS International Business School

Berivan Kul

Master Student, CBS International Business School

Key words : Holistic Worldview, Responsible Management Education, Sustainability Performance, Sustainable Key Competencies, Sustainable Development Goals, SDG Teaching Map

【Abstract】

Responsible management education is facing great challenges, and management scandals are increasing. Moreover, ecological and social concerns are often only half-heartedly integrated into business activities, and the only important factor ultimately is that profit is sufficient. Changes need time, which our world does not have, a shining example of which is the worldwide movement "Friday for Future." The mechanistic view of the world must be replaced by a more holistic worldview, which is where this paper comes in: how can responsible management education contribute, in order to consolidate this collaborative approach to integrate environmental and social issues in global supply chains? Based on different pedagogical approaches and the sustainability performance model, an SDG teaching map is developed herein, using the example of the CBS International Business School.

Responsible management education is on everyone's lips. In a global, increasingly complex and dynamic world, the development of which no longer corresponds to our linear models of thinking, the problems that need to be solved by politics, society and companies are manifold. Climate change, inhumane working conditions, lack of income, child labour – the list of environmental and social problems in the global supply chain grows almost daily, and so business schools must seize the responsibility for training the managers of the future. This paper has set itself the task of using a concrete example, namely the CBS International Business School, to explain its sustainability vision in terms of serving as a role model for other business schools. "Rethinking Capitalism" is one of the essential requirements for meeting the ecological and social challenges of our time. Based on this fundamental change in the understanding of business moving toward a more holistic approach, the idea of an SDG teaching map is discussed. The question to be answered is how a business school can contribute to the achievement of the Sustainable Development Goals (SDGs) through innovative teaching content and methods. This will be explained in concrete terms in the example of SDG 12, by building on pedagogical approaches and key competencies for sustainable management education. This conceptual paper concludes with a discussion of the implications this SDG teaching map approach can – and should – have for the curriculum design of a business school.

1. The CBS vision: a sustainable management approach

The CBS International Business School is a state-approved, private business school in Germany, which has recently completed a re-branding process, in order to bundle its strengths. Consequently, the two universities European Business School, in Mainz, and Cologne Business School, in Cologne, now appear under the joint name "CBS International Business School." In an increasingly connected and complex world, CBS wants to continue to combine education with personality, academic demands with practical relevance and an international community with individual support. CBS offers study programmes on all levels – Bachelor, Master, MBA as well as joint PHD programs with well-known international universities. In 2018, it was the first German university to receive the internationally renowned IACBE accreditation, and in December last year, it was awarded (for the third time in a row) Germany's best private Univer-

sity of Applied Sciences for Business Administration in the WirtschaftsWoche university ranking (CBS, 2020).

Following its mission "Creating Tomorrow," the CBS formulated a vision which places responsible business education at the heart of its research and teaching activities: "The CBS International Business School is developing into a respected international business school and one of the leading private universities in Europe. Our ambitious educational concept based on high quality and scientific competence in research and teaching meets this demand and is the basis for a substantial growth in our student numbers in the future. Employability and lifelong learning are very important at the CBS. We develop our students into competent and responsible decision-makers who take their social role seriously and find solutions for the economic problems of our time. The CBS is regarded as a pioneer of a new understanding of management. We support our students with a network of alumni and corporate partners in order to intensify the continuous exchange between practice, science and society" (CBS, 2020).

Responsible management education is thus firmly anchored in the self-image of the CBS teaching and research approach. Students are demanding new content in education, and the growing recognition among CEOs confirms that management education at business schools is becoming progressively more important. Only managers who have skills in sustainable management help companies to achieve their goals, not only in terms of cost optimisation, but especially also in terms of quality improvement and innovation (Kolb, Fröhlich, and Schmidpeter, 2017). For the challenges of our time, new solutions are needed, and to meet them accordingly one needs courage, vision and the will to work collaboratively (see also Chapter 2-3). This change from a mechanistic to a holistic worldview, in connection with the clear orientation of the CBS towards the Sustainable Development Goals in teaching and research, led to the idea of this paper and the development of an SDG teaching map. The academic debate is still largely focused on the justification of why sustainable development requires a broad adoption in management education. However, a concrete specification of how business schools could contribute to SDGs is still largely lacking, and this paper will at least provide an initial conceptual framework to answer this research need.

2. | Theoretical background

Recently, the researcher read the following quote by Wayne Visser (2020), and it seems very appropriate for characterising the problem of responsible management education. It is necessary to find innovative teaching approaches and also to rethink content that enables future managers to develop these 'fair and inclusive' solutions in a beneficial economic context: "How can we navigate through complexity? […] In today's world, it is not only the problems that are complex, but also the solutions – and the tide of (often contradictory) information adds to our bewilderment. There are two principles that I use like oars

to help steer me through complexity: First, the how is as important as the what; hence, is the proposed solution fair and inclusive? And second, the context is as important as the action; hence, what level of the system benefits or suffers?"

2-1. Rethinking capitalism: a holistic worldview for sustainable management education

This chapter provides a brief overview of a changing understanding of economics. For the last 500 years, the focus has been on breaking down complex problems into small, solvable parts in order to understand better and find solutions to these simple sub-problems, and this has come to be known as the *mechanistic worldview*. Adam Smith propagated the free market economy in this context. His so-called 'invisible hand' leads to the best possible allocation of resources and the highest possible level of prosperity in a society. It is often forgotten that the idea of the 'invisible hand' is based on the theory of moral sentiments (Smith, 2018), which means that this particular mechanism only works in an economic environment characterised by 'sympathy' and 'empathy.' Since this 'moral context' does not exist in our time, governments are expected to intervene, to counteract the market malfunctioning. To a certain extent, these regulations have also achieved considerable success, but there is no denying that government programmes are associated with a high degree of bureaucracy, ineffectiveness and, unfortunately, waste of resources (Fullerton, 2015).

It is precisely this problem that the *holistic*

worldview addresses, in that it "recognizes that the proper functioning of complex wholes (like an economy) cannot be understood without understanding the ongoing, dynamic relationship among parts that give rise to greater 'wholes'" (Fullerton, 2015, p. 8). The idea of holism was introduced by Jan Smuts (1926), who defined it as the tendency of nature to form the whole through creative evolution, which is more than the sum of its single parts. Holism is often also referred to as 'systems theory', whereby the whole system can only be understood if one grasps the relationship between all of the parts (Fullerton, 2015). Applied to our business context, managers who look at the economy in isolation from society and the biosphere ignore the damage that their behaviour might have on other parts of society and the environment. In order to avoid the previously discussed problems of the free market economy and the 'invisible hand', it is the task of a business school in teaching and research to facilitate this change from a competitive, mechanistic worldview to an ecological, collaborative worldview, also known as 'regenerative business models' (Brown et al., 2018).

2-2. Sustainable management education

After the Agenda 2030 for Sustainable Development was adopted, the importance of responsible management education and its potential for achieving SDGs was also widely recognised (Rieckmann, 2018). If this understanding is combined with the challenges of the holistic worldview explained in the previous section, it becomes clear that new educational approaches are needed. First, in this regard, the main pedagogical theories are briefly explained.

The three most relevant approaches are the learner-centred approach, experiential learning and transformative learning. The following explanations are taken from UNESCO (2017). The *learner-centred approach* describes the learner as autonomous and independent. Students themselves are responsible for their own learning progress, which gives them not only more power, but also responsibility, e.g. to suggest topics and methods that contribute to learning success. In the context of *experiential learning*, knowledge is not only conveyed, but learning is also understood as a process in which the student develops knowledge himself as the result of grasping and transforming experience. Experiential learning follows a cycle that begins with a concrete experience of the learner. By individually reflecting on this experience, and through observation, the learner formulates an abstract hypothesis, and this in turn leads to a new implication for action. These implications are tested and lead to new observations/experiences. The long-term goal of the *transformative learning approach* is to develop the learner into an autonomous thinker, while the short-term goal is to acquire specific competencies. These goals are achieved by distinguishing between 'habit of mind' (permanent, difficult to change) and 'points of view' (easier to change and therefore less permanent). The student learns to solve problems through critical reflection and communicative learning, and typical teaching methods, for example, are case studies, simulations or group projects.

All three theories are suitable for providing education for sustainable development. Traditional teaching methods, where the teacher speaks and the students' task is to listen, do not promote the acquisition of sustainable key competencies that play a central role in the sustainability performance model (Rieckmann, 2018), as discussed below.

The central task of this model is to explain how – in our context – managers can be enabled to change their behaviour and act in a way that promotes sustainable development. Two key requirements must be taken into account in this case. On the one hand, relevant issues relating to sustainable management must be integrated into teaching, and innovative teaching methods have to be used, in line with the comments just made on the most important pedagogical theories for sustainable development (Rieckmann, 2018).

'Knowledge and skills' and 'sustainable key competencies' are shown in Figure 1 and represent the two key requirements just mentioned. Fundamentally, it is posited that the sustainability performance of a manager can be described according to four dimensions. The acquisition of relevant knowledge and skills, as well as relevant key competencies for coping with complex sustainability problems, have already been named. Since competencies alone are not sufficient to determine a corresponding sustainable action, values and motivation play an important role in this model, since they translate the ability to act sustainably in a concrete activity. Last but not least, sustainability performance is defined by

Figure1　Key competencies and performance of sustainability citizens

Source: Rieckmann (2018, p.46).

the individual environment of the manager, whilst 'opportunities' describe factors that cannot be controlled by the manager himself. Contextual and environmental mechanisms make concrete sustainable measures possible (Rieckmann, 2018).

This model serves as the basis for outlining the further steps required to establish the SDG teaching map. Sustainable key competencies, which will be explained in more detail in the next section, and the question regarding which skills necessary to accomplish the SDGs can be anchored in a business school curriculum, should be discussed first. In addition, there is the problem that key competencies are not part of formal education at universities, and the integration of so-called 'soft skills' has reached its limit, particularly due to the restrictive requirements of accreditation bodies. 'Values and motivation' are achieved through the use of new teaching formats, which is why the relevant pedagogical theories have been described above. In business

Figure 2   Key sustainable competencies

Systems thinking competency Recognizing and understanding relationships and complex systems in a certain context.	**Collaboration competency** Learning from others, collaborative problem solving, dealing with conflicts in groups, understanding each other.
Anticipatory competency Understanding and evaluating different futures; assessing risks and consequences of actions.	**Critical thinking competency** Ability to critically reflect on values, actions, opinions.
Normative competency Understand and reflect on norms/values; understand actions/make trade-offs embedded in a value system.	**Self-awareness competency** Understand and reflect on one's own role, feelings, actions.
Strategic competency Innovative action to enable sustainable development.	**Integrated problem-solving competency** Apply problem-solving methods and find solutions promoting sustainability.

Source: Rieckmann (2018, pp.44-45).

projects, for example, where students work on specific company tasks, these values and attitudes of future managers can be sharpened (more examples can be found in section 4). 'Opportunities' result from the research activities undertaken at CBS, and the collaborative investigation of innovative but practice-relevant sustainable questions with students enables them to prepare for the challenges of their future work and provides initial insights into what tasks and challenges will need to be mastered in management in the future. At the same time, students are equipped with the necessary toolbox for sustainable management.

2-3. Sustainable key competencies and performance

In this subsection, a short overview of possible key competencies, which are briefly described in Figure 2, will be given. Since the concept of key competencies is only one of the four dimensions in the sustainability performance model, this brief description is sufficient. Competencies can be described as 'the ability to apply learning outcomes adequately in a defined context (education, work, personal, or professional development)' (European Centre for the Development of Vocational Training, 2008, p.47). A distinction must be made between different competencies, and in addition to the key skills there exist also general and specific cognitive abilities. It is important to note that neither key competencies nor specific cognitive competencies alone induce the desired sustainable management behaviour (Weinert, 2001). For this reason, it is important that a curriculum for the sustainable management of a business school considers both dimensions of the model at hand (Figure 1), i.e. sustainable key competencies, and knowledge and skills, for only in their interplay can the necessary behaviour be achieved to solve complex sustainability problems in management. Figure 2 illustrates a short discussion of the eight relevant key sustainable competency areas.

The importance of key competencies will be illustrated using a specific example. The sustainable design of global supply chains is one of the greatest current corporate challenges. In order to evaluate and develop suppliers in terms of a company's sustainability vision, *collaboration competence* is particularly necessary. Joint problem-solving, in the sense of fair supplier management aiming to achieve common goals, is an indispensable prerequisite for attaining sustainability goals in the supply chain, whilst *normative competence*, understood as intercultural abilities, is also essential. For example, auditing processes in certain cultures can lead to mistrust of the purchasing company and make the successful implementation of ecological and social standards in the supply chain more difficult. The *ability to reflect critically* on one's own behaviour and that of the supplier company, and thus to place values, activities and opinions in the right context, is a key factor in the success of a buyer-supplier relationship (Fröhlich and Steinbiss, 2018).

3. The Sustainable Development Goal (SDG) teaching map

In summary, sustainable companies have more than the sole purpose of creating shareholder value, only taking financial information into account and then strategising accordingly; furthermore, sustainable companies do not simply engage in philanthropic activities. Sustainable business serves all relevant stakeholders, with information on environmental, social and economic issues being given equal consideration in any corporate strategy. The

focus falls on creating shared value in operations throughout the entire value chain, and so responsible management requires leadership that acquires the necessary skills and knowledge to make this vision a reality and works towards a more holistic economic worldview.

3-1. A process for establishing the SDG teaching map

The SDG teaching map presented in this paper was developed in a Master thesis at the CBS International Business School (Kul, 2020). In a first step, the research process is briefly outlined. Referring to this first step, SDG 12 and its sub-goals are explained, in order to understand the evaluation made in the last section of this chapter.

The previous paragraphs form the theoretical basis of the development process. It was necessary to explain the challenges responsible management education has to face and which pedagogical theories can be applied to impart the necessary competencies. The model of sustainability performance summarises the relevant dimensions that ultimately enable managers to implement necessary sustainable strategies and measures. In the next step, the curricula of all English-language programs at CBS International Business School were analysed. On the basis of this analysis, it was possible to determine which sub-goals of the 17 SDGs are covered, and in which lectures these subjects can be found. The data collected in this way were verified by the results of a focus group conducted online. Three specific questions were asked: (a) Which con-

Figure 3   Research process for establishing the SDG teaching map

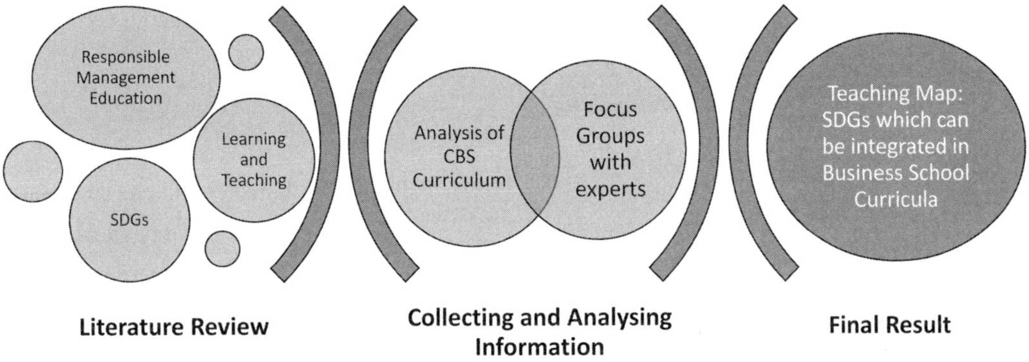

Source: Own illustration.

tents of the 17 SDGs sub-targets that have not been covered so far could be integrated into the curriculum of a business school? (b) How could these contents be integrated (e.g. establish a new lecture or integrate them into existing lectures)? (c) Which contents of the sub-goals of the 17 SDGs cannot be represented by a business school? How could they be acquired? This part of the research process to deduct the SDG teaching map will not be considered further in this paper, due to word count limitations.

The SDG teaching map, shown in Figure 4, is the final result of this research process. Chapter 4 provides concluding suggestions on how a business school can further improve its curriculum in terms of responsible management education.

3-2. The SDG teaching map: the SDG 12 case

So far, this paper has dealt with the 'how?' of responsible management education, so this section shall now address the content, i.e. the 'what?' Since responsible management education is aimed at supporting the sustainable de-velopment of society, the orientation of this research project towards the Sustainable Development Goals can be justified. The most critical fields of action were set by the United Nations in the definition of the 17 SDGs: "The 2030 Agenda for Sustainable Development, adopted by all United Nations Member States in 2015, provides a shared blueprint for peace and prosperity for people and the planet, now and into the future. At its heart are the 17 Sustainable Development Goals (SDGs), which are an urgent call for action by all countries – developed and developing – in a global partnership. They recognize that ending poverty and other deprivations must go hand-in-hand with strategies that improve health and education, reduce inequality, and spur economic growth – all while tackling climate change and working to preserve our oceans and forests" (United Nations, 2020b). These contents are considered essential for teaching, to enable students to lead society towards a sustainable future. Therefore, the literature (Rieckmann, 2018) also recommends their integration into the curriculum of a business school. SDG 12 and its sub-goals are briefly explained below, because it serves as an example to explain the SDG teaching map.

The goal of *SDG 12 'Responsible Consumption and Production'* (United Nations, 2020a) addresses both consumers and companies. On the one hand, it deals with the sustainable consumption of products or services, and especially analysing and adapting consumption patterns in developing countries are of particular relevance. On the other hand, SDG 12 addresses sustainable production, which includes the entire supply chain directed to the supply market. What is special about SDG 12 is that progress in this area also has a positive impact on other SDGs in their achievement of objectives. At the same time, it has to consider the most relevant entrepreneurial challenges, such as resources not being used efficiently and the material footprint continuing to increase, because consumption patterns are difficult to change. SDG 12 illustrates more than any other SDG how important responsible management education is. Managers need tangible instructions on how to deal with the environmental and social impacts of production and consumption. Circular economy or regenerative business models are management approaches that need to be implemented to achieve the goal of SDG 12, which covers the following sub-targets (sub-targets 12a to 12c are not considered herein):

"12.1 Implement the 10-year framework of programs on sustainable consumption and production, all countries taking action, with developed countries taking the lead, taking into account the development and capabilities of developing countries

12.2 By 2030, achieve the sustainable management and efficient use of natural resources

12.3 By 2030, halve per capita global food waste at the retail and consumer levels and reduce food losses along production and supply chains, including post-harvest losses

12.4 By 2020, achieve the environmentally sound management of chemicals and all wastes throughout their life cycle, in accordance with agreed international frameworks, and significantly reduce their release to air, water and soil in order to minimize their adverse impacts on human health and the environment

12.5 By 2030, substantially reduce waste generation through prevention, reduction, recycling and reuse

12.6 Encourage companies, especially large and transnational companies, to adopt sustainable practices and to integrate sustainability information into their reporting cycle

12.7 Promote public procurement practices that are sustainable, in accordance with national policies and priorities

12.8 By 2030, ensure that people everywhere have the relevant information and awareness for sustainable development and lifestyles in harmony with nature" (United Nations, 2020a, N.P.)

As Figure 4 illustrates, only one of the SDG 12 sub-goals is not addressed, namely sub-goal

Figure 4   The SDG teaching map

Source: Own illustration.

12.7, which deals with sustainable public procurement. In principle, there is little content in the CBS curriculum that relates to public administration topics.

It can be stated that SDG 12 'Responsible Consumption and Production' is *one of the best-anchored SDGs in the CBS curriculum*; for example, the lecture Sustainable Supply Chain Management (SSCM) is held in both the Master and Bachelor programmes and designed in line with the educational approach of experiential learning, particularly in the Master's programme. Students are motivated to develop solutions to current sustainability topics in the supply chain, together with experts and the responsible lecturer. Topics that have been worked on in the past semesters include regenerative business models, waste management, sustainable consumer behaviour or sustainable procurement and logistics solutions (SDGs 12.2–12.6). Due to a joint

project with GIZ (Gesellschaft für Internationale-Zusammenarbeit), sustainable agricultural supply chains are currently the focus of teaching and research tasks in this course (SDG 12.1). In the winter semester 2019, the results of the papers from the course Sustainable Supply Chain Management were summarised and published in a Working Paper. The results are available to students in subsequent semesters and can thus be used as an example for the learning cycle in experiential learning. Sub-goal 12.8, which supports sustainable communication strategies and reporting, is addressed in the lectures SSCM, Communication Policy and International Marketing.

In order to give a first impression, a short overview is provided on the basis of the Master programme International Business, the lectures for which contain contents of SDG 12: Business Economics, Corporate Social Responsibility, Special Issues in Globalisation, Global and Industrial Corporate Social Responsibility, Digital Strategising, Sustainable Supply Chain Management, Market Innovation or Entrepreneurship in a social context. This list illustrates the idea behind the integrated sustainability curriculum (Kolb, Fröhlich, and Schmidpeter, 2017), which has been successfully implemented at CBS in recent years. Besides basic lectures on CSR, different applications thereof can be found, such as Social Innovation or SSCM, or sustainability aspects are integrated in lectures with no specific sustainability focus at all, such as Market Innovation or Digital Strategising.

Particularly noteworthy are the *business projects*, as part of the innovative building block, in which students work on specific tasks set by companies. Currently, three projects contributing to SDG 12's sub-goals are being worked on: developing a global market entry strategy for a company in the food industry, the calculation of the carbon footprint for the last mile logistics of a publishing house and implementing a sustainable communication concept for a large German trading company; the business projects thus fall under the transformative learning approach. Students are encouraged to become autonomous thinkers and improve their skills through critical reflection and communicative learning, and the results are repeatedly discussed and improved in feedback rounds with lecturers and company representatives.

A few years ago, the CBS International Business School established a student consultancy, the *conCBS*, which also uses the transformative learning approach. Here, the students work in a consulting setting on topics that can also be assigned to SDG 12, e.g. the development of a sustainable procurement strategy for one of the main German energy suppliers.

4. │ Next steps: how to improve sustainable management education

Following the procedure described in the previous chapter, all 17 SDGs were analysed accordingly. The SDG teaching map has some gaps, which now need to be closed in a next step. Coming back to the results from the focus group design, the first hints are given on how to improve the achievement of the SDGs through adequate teaching methods and content. The most important learnings can be summarised as follows:

- It was possible to identify the teaching content that can be integrated into the curriculum of a business school.
- Sustainable teaching content was identified from other disciplines that should be included in a future management curriculum, e.g. urban planning, smart cities or environmental science.
- The remaining white spots of the SDG teaching map have to be developed in cooperation with institutional or practice partners.

Finally, three ideas for the expansion of the current curriculum of the CBS International Business School need to be explained, but these will have to be worked out in more detail in the further course of the research work in this field.

In the previous chapter, it was explained that SDG 12.7 *Sustainable Public Procurement* is not part of the CBS curriculum, but this problem can be solved very easily, in that an independent elective course can be considered, as this topic is currently also of great importance in practice. As lectures on the topic of procurement management are integrated into all CBS programmes, sustainable public procurement content can also be included in these courses.

The *sustainable design of agricultural supply chains* is the focus of the Initiative for Sustainable Agricultural Supply Chains (INA), a working group of the GIZ (Gesellschaft für InternationaleZusammenarbeit) (INA, 2020). It was recognised by those responsible that cooperation with a business school is necessary, as for this task purchasers who require special training in the field of sustainable agricultural supply chains are targeted. Since this qualification does not exist on the personnel market, the INA has set up a programme together with the Federal Ministry for International Cooperation (BMIZ). Master students of German universities are invited to take part at a three-day seminar in Berlin, at the end of which they write a paper on a given relevant topic. Fourteen students who have written the best papers are then invited to Ghana for one week, at the expense of the BMIZ, to experience in real life what they have researched in theory. The results will be used to develop a new Master course format.

One of the previous lessons learned was that there are certain sustainable topics that cannot be integrated into the curriculum of a business school. A *summer school* offered for students who are very interested in the topic of sustainable management could be a promising idea and be facilitated through three or four international partners on topics that are not offered at the chosen partner university. Possible topics could be sustainable fashion, carbon literacy training, environmental science or urban planning. Students would choose a topic during each summer break and receive an additional certificate after successful participation in three modules. This would make it possible, through cooperation with universities from other disciplines, to teach sustainable subject matter that would not ordinarily find a place on an economic curriculum.

In summary, a more comprehensive responsible management curriculum is needed to solve the previously discussed entrepreneurial challenges related to ecological and social problems.

〈References〉
Brown, M., Haselsteiner, E., Apró, D., Kopeva, D., Luca, E., Pulkkinen, K. and Vula Rizvanolli, B. (Eds.) (2018) *Sustainability, Restorative and Regenerative*, Available at https://www.eurestore.eu/wp-content/uploads/2018/04/Sustainability-Restorative-to-Regenerative.pdf, Accessed February 20th 2020.

CBS International Business School (2020) Available at https://cbs.de/en/advice-admission/ten-good-reasons, Accessed February 20th 2020.

European Centre for the Development of Vocational Training (Ed.) (2008) *Terminology of European education and training policy: A selection of 100 key terms*, Luxembourg: Office for Official Publications of the European Communities.

Fröhlich, E. and Steinbiss, K. (2018) 'Die Integration der "Sustainable Development Goals" in eine nachhaltige Supply Chain' (The Integration of SDGs into a Sustainable Supply Chain): Der "Nachhaltige

Beschaffungs-Case" (The Sustainable Procurement Case)', in Wellenbrock, W. *Nachhaltige Beschaffung (Sustainable Procurement)*, pp. 37-54, Wiesbaden: Springer.

Fullerton, J. (2015) *Regenerative Capitalism*, Capital Institute, org.

INA (2020) Available at https://www.nachhaltige-agrarlieferketten.org, Accessed February 20th 2020.

Kolb, M., Fröhlich, L. and Schmidpeter, R. (2017) 'Implementing sustainability as the new normal: Responsible management education – From a private business school's perspective, *The International Journal of Management Education*, Vol. 15, No. 2, pp. 280-292.

Kul, B. (2020) *Responsible Management Education: Implementing the Sustainable Development Goals into Business School Curricula*, unpublished Master Thesis, Cologne, CBS International Business School.

Rieckmann, M. (2018) 'Learning to transform the world: key competencies in Education for Sustainable Development', in Leicht, A., Heiss, J., and Byun, W.J. (Eds.), *Issues and trends in Education for Sustainable Development*, pp. 38-59, Available at https://www.rri-tools.eu/-/issues-and-trends-in-education-for-sustainable-development, Accessed February 20th 2020.

Smith, A. (2018) *The Theory of Moral Sentiments*, Stilwell: Digireads.

Smuts, J. (1926) *Holism and Evolution*, New York: Macmillan & Company Limited.

UNESCO (2017) *Education for sustainable development goals: Learning objectives*, Available at https://unesdoc.unesco.org/ark:/48223/pf0000247444, Accessed February 20th 2020.

United Nations (2020a) *Goal 12: Ensure sustainable consumption and production patterns*, Available at https://www.un.org/sustainabledevelopment/sustainable-consumption-production, Accessed February 20th 2020.

—— (2020b) *Sustainable Development Goals*, Available at https://sustainabledevelopment.un.org/sdgs, Accessed February 20th 2020.

Visser, W. (2020) Purpose Inspired Daily Reflection: #Complexity, Accessed January 30th 2020.

Weinert, F.E. (2001) 'Concept of competence: A conceptual clarification', in Rychen, D.S. and Salganik, L.H. (Eds.), *Defining and selecting key competencies*, pp. 45-65, Ashland: Hogrefe & Huber Publishers.

企業と社会フォーラム学会誌，第 9 号，pp. 33-41, 2020　　33

サステナブルビジネス教育における課題
——トランスフォーメーションの時代に求められるもの

関　正雄

損害保険ジャパン CSR 室シニアアドバイザー

明治大学経営学部特任教授

キーワード：SDGs（持続可能な開発目標），サステナブルビジネス教育，トランスフォーメーション，イノベーション，バックキャスティング，Society 5.0 for SDGs，スウェーデンの CSR 政策，中国の政策決定者への教育，市民教育，ESD（持続可能な発展のための教育）

【要旨】

　SDGs 達成のためには漸進的改善では足りず，社会・経済をシステムレベルで大変革するトランスフォーメーションが必要である。ひとつのカギを握るのはデジタル・トランスフォーメーションであろう。企業はその原動力というべき存在であり，バックキャスティング思考でイノベーションを創出する人材を育てる必要がある。さらに，人材育成にはビジネス・パーソンへの教育だけではなく，政策決定者向けの同趣旨の教育も極めて重要であり，スウェーデンや中国の事例はこの点において参考にすべきである。また，社会の大変革を求めて政府や企業に対して意思表示する，成熟した市民社会の存在も欠かせない。SDGs をきっかけに，社会におけるサステナビリティ主流化のために現在の教育のどこをどう変えるべきか，改めて検討する必要がある。

1.　企業戦略としての教育

1-1. SDGs の時代に求められる企業の役割とは

　企業として CSR（企業の社会的責任）を推進するうえで，欠かせないのが教育である。いうまでもなく，企業にとって「CSR イコール CSR 部門の仕事」なのではなく，経営層から第一線の社員にまで，そして経営戦略から日々の業務に至るまで，あらゆる部署の意思決定や活動に組み込まれ，事業活動と一体化（統合）されていなければならない。そのためには，知識を身に付けるだけではなく，共感し行動するレベルにまで社員全員に CSR 教育を徹底する必要がある。

　そして，教育が効果をあげるためには，組織としてのビジョンの確立と共有，および計画を遂行するための実効的なマネジメントシステムの存在が前提である。つまり，CSR 推進に必要なのは，ビジョン，システム，教育の 3 要素であって，このいずれが欠けても本物にはならない。いわば 3 要素の足し算ではなく掛け算である。たとえば如何に立派なビジョンやシステムがあっても，CSR を正しく理解し，自分で考えて行動する社員がいなければ，CSR は文字通り「絵に描いた餅」になってしまう。

　現代の企業にとって，CSR 教育の重要なテーマのひとつは，SDGs（持続可能な開発目標）で

あろう。SDGsの本質的理解を浸透させることは，社会における企業の存在意義やCSRの重要性を深く考えさせることに役立つ。その意味で，SDGsは社員教育における重要なテーマであり，有効なツールでもある。

SDGsがその前身であるMDGs（ミレニアム開発目標）と大きく違うのは，SDGsの達成に不可欠な存在として，企業が力を発揮することが大いに期待されている点である。また実際に国内外の多くの企業がSDGsを事業そのものに組み込むべく，つまり経営戦略に統合すべく取り組んでいる。

なお，こうした，ブームとまで言えるほど急激に進む企業へのSDGs浸透の動きのなかでも，これまでに確立されたCSRの基本概念が変わったわけでも時代遅れになったわけでもないことは念のために強調しておきたい。SDGsが目指している持続可能で包摂的な社会の実現には，社会・経済のルールから人々の価値観・行動に至るまで，システムレベルでの大きな変革（トランスフォーメーション）が必要とされる。そして大きな変革の時代は，企業にとっては大きなビジネスチャンスの到来を意味する。その点が「オポチュニティとしてのSDGs」に企業が着目する理由となっている。しかし，こうした動機から企業にとって好都合ないいとこどり（チェリーピッキング）をするだけでは，批判の対象にされかねない。企業は自然資本や社会資本に依存し，また同時にインパクトを与えており，そのインパクトはポジティブとネガティブの両面があること，したがってSDGsに取り組むうえでも正と負との両面で自社と社会との関係をみていかなければならないことを，忘れてはならない。たとえば環境汚染や人権侵害など自らがもたらす恐れのある負の影響に対処することはCSRの基本であり，同時に重要なSDGsの要請であることを理解しておく必要

がある。この点は，SDGsに取り組む企業向けのガイドとして最も一般的な，SDGsコンパスでも強調されているところである。

1-2. イノベーション人材を育てる必要性

以上を前提として，SDGsの時代に企業が何を求められているのか，ビジネス教育や人材育成の観点から考察していくこととする。

キーワードは未来志向，戦略思考であり，SDGs達成へのアプローチとしてのバックキャスティングである。このことは，SDGsの目標13（気候変動との戦い）を例に考えるとよくわかる。全世界で自治体・都市をはじめとするさまざまな主体が切迫感をもって気候非常事態宣言を発しているとおり，破滅的事態を回避するために人類に残された時間はわずかである。企業も含めすべてのステークホルダーが，これまでの取り組みの延長線上で目標を設定するフォアキャスティングのアプローチからの脱却を求められている。

企業においても，将来の大きな変化を見通したうえでの計画と行動が求められている。科学的知見をベースにして気候変動対策の目標設定と行動を求めるSBT（サイエンス・ベースド・ターゲット）の動きや，シナリオ分析に基づく自社の中長期的な気候変動戦略を財務情報として投資家に開示することを推奨するTCFD（気候関連財務情報開示に関するタスクフォース）の動きなどが，そのよい例である。いずれも，中長期的に脱炭素社会に向けて大変化する社会を想定し，外部環境起点で戦略を描いて設定した目標を，達成状況とともにステークホルダーに開示することが要請されているのである。

ここでは，過去から現在までの実績の延長線上で未来社会を描くのではなく，パリ協定で国際合意となった達成すべき長期目標に向けて時代を先取りし社会変革の力となることが要請さ

れている。SDGs の本質は，持続不可能な現代社会を何とか持続可能な社会へと変容（トランスフォーム）させるために，社会・経済システムを大改革することが不可欠であることを訴えたものであり，故に破壊的なイノベーションをもたらすことができる企業の力が重要とされているのである。企業は，SDGs が必要とする大きな変革へのダイナミズムを経営戦略に組み込んで，自社の企業価値向上にいかにつなげるかが問われている。そこでは，これまでにない長期視点でシナリオ分析を行い，バックキャスティングで目標を設定し，自社戦略に落とし込むことのできる，新たな人材スペックのイノベーション人材が求められているのである。

1-3. 経団連が進める Society 5.0 for SDGs

　産業界自身もこうした新たな変化を行動規範に取り込む動きがある。2017 年に経団連が行った企業行動憲章の大幅な改定では，SDGs 達成のために企業が果たすべき，イノベーションを創出する役割を強調している。今回の憲章改定の主眼は，会員企業に SDGs への取り組みを強く促すことにあった。そこで，憲章のサブタイトルを「持続可能な発展のために」と書き換え，前文でも「企業は持続可能な社会の実現を牽引する役割を担う（下線は筆者）」，と明確に言い切っている[1]。

　また，より具体的な戦略として，企業行動憲章実行の手引きにおいて「Society 5.0 for SDGs」という経団連オリジナルの戦略を提言している。Society 5.0 は，2016 年に閣議決定された日本政府の戦略であり，実現すべき近未来社会である。革新的なデジタル技術も活用して，一人ひとりの異なるニーズにキメ細かく対応し，かつ社会全体を最適化する，ひと言でいえば人間中心の超スマート社会を指す。この「Society5.0 の実現を通じて SDGs の達成に貢献する」ことに企業は大きな貢献ができるし自身の価値向上にもつなげることができる，というのが経団連の提唱する，デジタル・トランスフォーメーションを中核とした Society 5.0 for SDGs 戦略である。

　経団連では，会員企業に新たな憲章・実行の手引きの浸透を図り，また国内外への Society 5.0 for SDGs 戦略の発信を強化するため，イノベーション事例を企業から収集したり，日本での G20 に先立って 2019 年 3 月に東京で開催された B20 において政策提言の柱と位置付けるなどして，推進に力を入れている。

2. サステナビリティ政策としての教育

2-1. スウェーデンのサステナビリティ政策

　本節では，サステナブルな社会の構築を目指して政策に力を入れており実際に国際的な評価も高い北欧諸国に焦点を当てる。スウェーデンを例に取れば，独エーデルマン財団が毎年発表している SDGs の国別ランキング[2]で 2018 年は世界 1 位，2019 年もデンマークに次いで 2 位と高い評価を受けている。

　スウェーデンは，人口約 1,000 万人で国内市場もさほど大きくないので，成長戦略の中心はイノベーションと輸出振興である。そのため研究開発への投資にも積極的で，グローバル・イノベーション・インデックスでは，スイスに次いで 129 ヵ国中 2 位と高く評価されている[3]。国の政策とも相まって IKEA や H&M などスウェーデン企業はグローバル市場を見据えた戦略を遂行しており，国際競争力の重要な要素としてサステナビリティに力を入れている。

　スウェーデンの NGO ナチュラルステップが提唱したバックキャスティングアプローチは，スウェーデン政府の環境政策の基本に取り入れられている。例えば，2045 年には世界各国に

先駆けて脱化石燃料の国にするとの長期計画を明らかにし，そのためのロードマップも，コンクリート，食料，森林，鉄，海洋，デジタル化，などの各分野に関して策定している。また，ストックホルム市内の再開発地域，ロイヤル・シーポート地区では，モデル地区としてさらに前倒しし2030年までに脱炭素を実現することをめざしている。

スウェーデンは，こうした一連の政策の実際の効果として，経済成長を実現しつつ他方でCO_2排出を削減するという，いわゆるデカップリングを成功させている。1990年からのGDPは3倍に拡大する一方で，温室効果ガス排出は同期間で24%削減しているのである[4]。そして，グローバルな企業の競争力と国の競争力に直結するCSRは重要政策イシューであると捉え，官民一体となって世界戦略に組み込んでいる。そのひとつの表れが，CSRを外務省が所管していることであろう。

スウェーデン政府は外務省にCSR大使を置いているほか，大使館でのCSRに関する活動にも力を入れている。スウェーデン政府は，中国政府との間で2007年と2009年に結んだCSRに関する協力覚書（MOU）に基づき，日本のJICAに相当するスウェーデンの国際協力機関SIDAを通じて，10年間にわたり中国の地方政府職員のCSR教育支援に取り組んできた。また，北京のスウェーデン大使館には2010年にCSRセンターを設置して，中国で開催されるCSRの国際フォーラムに，大使館職員やスウェーデン企業を数多く登壇させている。この中国に対する一連のCSR支援政策は，中国政府のCSR人材育成に資する国際協力の形をとっているが，同時にスウェーデン企業の中国市場への進出の足がかりをつくり地ならしをする意義があり，同国企業の中国市場での優位性を高めるというグローバル戦略の一環

でもあると理解できよう。

2-2. 中国におけるCSR教育

中国では，政府主導でCSRの推進が行われている。2015年には，ISO26000をベースに開発した中国独自のCSRの国家規格GB/T36000シリーズが発行され，体系的なCSR基準が確立された。同規格は，社会的責任のガイダンス，レポーティング，評価基準の三部作からなる国家標準であり，世界の基準と整合するCSRの国内共通言語を樹立したことの意義は大きい。

また，中央企業（中央政府直属の主要国有企業）にはサステナビリティレポート発行を義務付けるなど率先してCSRに取り組むように促し，外資企業にはグローバル水準の先進的な取り組みを中国でも期待し，地方の国有企業にも広く浸透させるため地方政府におけるCSRの理解を促進させることに力を入れる。上場企業に対しては，証券取引所がCSR報告を要請する。このようにさまざまなチャネルを通じてCSRの浸透を政策的に図ってきた。責任競争力という言葉がよく使われるのも，国際競争に晒される中国企業の競争力に関わる問題としてCSRを捉えているからである。これらの政策の効果として，中国でのCSRレポート発行企業数は増加を続け，2006年の33社から今や2000社をはるかに上回るほどまでになっている。

こうした政策意図の下でのCSRの普及に重要な役割を果たしてきたのが，商務部系雑誌社が発行する2002年創刊の月刊誌，WTO経済導刊（現在の名称はサステナビリティ経済導刊）である。国内外の最新のCSRの動向解説や評論，先進企業の取り組み事例などを伝え，CSRの啓発・普及に大きく貢献してきた。

WTO経済導刊を長く率いて，GB/T 36000

図1　中国の CSR 教育

1. 政府機関向け教育
   ・スウェーデン政府の支援による地方政府機関の職員，商工会議所の職員等への研修
   ・民間コンサルティング会社による中央政府職員，地方政府職員への CSR 教育　　など
2. 企業向けの教育
   ・SASAC（国務院国有資産監督管理委員会）による中央企業への CSR 教育
   ・地方国有資産監督管理委員会による地方国有企業への CSR 教育
   ・業界団体による傘下企業の CSR 教育
   ・民間コンサルティング会社によるセミナー・教育　　など
3. ビジネススクールや大学における CSR 教育
   ・2007 年以降，ビジネススクールの教員向けの，企業倫理と CSR 教育スキルに関する教育コースに 1,100 人が参加。
   ・2018 年には，企業倫理と CSR が MBA コースの必須科目に指定された。
   ・2008 年以降，100 以上の大学で企業倫理と CSR のコースが開講され，10 万人の学生が受講した。

出所：JFBS の第 9 回年次大会，Sustainability Leadership Training のセッションでの殷格非氏のプレゼンテーションから（2019 年 9 月 6 日）。

シリーズの策定にも関わり，現在は CSR の教育・コンサルティング会社である GoldenBee 社の設立人兼チーフエキスパートを務める殷格非氏によれば，中国における CSR 教育プログラムは，政策決定者，企業幹部，大学生などを対象に計画的に順次強化されてきており，その実績の主なものは図 1 にかかげるとおりである[(5)]。

欧州と中国との緊密な関係に関していえば，前出のスウェーデン政府以外にも，ドイツ政府からも国際協力機関 GIZ を通じての CSR 啓発・普及の支援[(6)]を受けながら，企業の能力構築に政策的・計画的に取り組んできた。中国の CSR は，北京・上海など中核都市や国有企業など大企業は別として，全国的にみればまだ発展途上である。とはいえ，CSR 教育を担う人材の育成を含む，こうした計画的・体系的な CSR 政策と CSR 教育の継続が実を結びつつあることは確かである。

SDGs の時代，目標達成のために求められるシステムレベルの変革には，スウェーデンの例にみられるように，明確な政策メッセージを示して大きく舵をとる政府の役割と強いリーダーシップが不可欠である。企業におけるイノベーション人材の育成が課題であるのと同様に，中央政府や地方自治体においても，これまでにない長期視点でシナリオ分析やバックキャスティングができ，そこからサステナビリティ政策に落とし込むことのできる，イノベーション人材が強く求められていることを指摘しておきたい。

3.　SDGs と市民社会の成熟

3-1.　気候変動への危機感の差

科学技術振興機構（JST）の調査結果が示す，気候変動に関する世界と日本の市民意識の鮮明な違いは興味深い。

図 2，図 3 が示すように，世界の市民の 79％が気候変動の影響をとても心配しているのに対して，日本の市民では，その割合は 44％に過ぎない。また，世界の市民の 66％が気候変動対策は生活の質を高めるものであると考えるのに対して，日本の市民の 60％は逆に生活の質を脅かすものと考えている。この調査結果は，日本の市民意識と行動レベルでの課題を考えるうえで，ヒントを与えてくれる。

例えば，危機感が特に強い欧州では 2019 年の欧州議会選挙で気候変動政策が選挙のイシューになり，若い世代の支持を背景に，環境

図2 「気候変動の影響」に対する危機感の違い

気候変動の影響について、日本市民は世界市民と比較すると「とても心配している」という割合が顕著に低い。

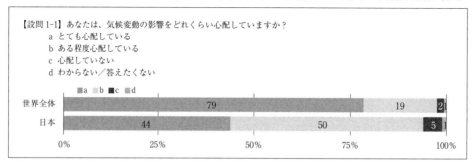

出所：World Wide Views on Climate and Energy
　　　世界市民会議「気候変動とエネルギー」開催報告書　平成 27 年 7 月　科学技術振興機構。

図3 「気候変動対策が及ぼす生活の質への影響」の受け止め方の違い

世界市民の多くは先進国を含め気候変動対策により「生活の質が高まる」と認識しているが、
日本市民の多くは「生活の質が脅かされる」と認識している。

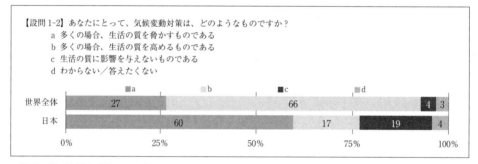

出所：World Wide Views on Climate and Energy
　　　世界市民会議「気候変動とエネルギー」開催報告書　平成 27 年 7 月　科学技術振興機構。

政策を重視する GREEEN/EFA 緑 / 欧州自由同盟の統一会派が躍進した。一方で，2019 年の台風災害や，毎年のように繰り返し豪雨・洪水災害に晒されている日本の国民は，それでも気候変動への危機感が強くないし，気候変動の緩和策は全くと言ってよいほど選挙の争点にはなっていない。

スウェーデンの国会議事堂前で，気候政策に本気で取り組まない政治家に抗議してストライキを始めた高校生のグレタ・トゥーンベリさんは，今や世界中の若者の共感を得てシンボル的存在となっている。世界の至るところで 700 万人以上もの若者が抗議行動に立ち上がっているなかで，日本の若者の参加は数千人といわれ，極めて少ない。

民主主義社会において，政策への意思表示とは結局のところ有権者の声である。サステナブルな社会の実現を望む，成熟した意識の高い市民が，有権者として，消費者として，政府や企業の行動に大きな影響力を及ぼす。例えば，スウェーデンの選挙の投票率は高い。2018 年の総選挙では，全年代の投票率は 87.18％，若者（18 歳から 29 歳）の投票率も約 85％と，いずれも日本とは比較にならないほどの高さである。スウェーデンの政府や企業の先進的な取り組みの原動力は市民の大きな声であり，こうした市

図4　グッドライフ目標から（一部抜粋）

貧困をなくす力になろう

1. 自分の国や海外の貧困の原因について学ぼう
2. できることを分かち合い寄付しよう
3. 公正な賃金・労働条件を満たした企業の製品を買おう
4. 貯金，借金，投資には責任を持とう
5. すべての人に対する適切な賃金と機会を要求しよう

よりよい食生活をしよう

1. 農業，漁業，食物生産について学ぼう
2. 果物や野菜をもっと食べよう
3. 地元のもの，旬のもの，公正な取引が行われた食品を買おう
4. 子ども，お年寄り，妊娠中の女性が健全な食生活を実践するための力になろう
5. 世界の飢餓をなくすよう要求しよう

健康に過ごそう

1. 健康でいるための方法を学び，分かち合おう
2. 手を洗い，定期的に運動をしよう
3. 路上やその付近では安全を保とう
4. 心身の健康と幸せを大切にしよう
5. すべての人に対する医療と予防接種を要求しよう

出所：World Business Council for Sustainable Development *"SDG Business Hub"*
　　　https://sdghub.com/goodlifegoals/

民を育むために必要なのは市民教育である。

3-2. 社会変革を求める市民とサステナブルビジネス

スウェーデンの学校教育のなかで市民参加や選挙権行使についてどう教えているかを知るためには，小学校や中学校の教科書がよい手掛かりとなる。一貫して教え込まれているのは，ひと言でいえば「社会は自分たちの手で変えられる」というモノの考え方である。

解決したい課題があったら，放置したりあきらめたりするのではなく，解決のために誰を巻き込んでどう行動すべきかを，デモ行進をしたりSNSを活用することの勧めも含め，すでに小学校の段階から教えている[7]。また，中学校の教科書のタイトルが「あなた自身の社会」であることも興味深い[8]。

日本ではどうであろうか。選挙の投票率がスウェーデンに比べて低いことに加え，サステナビリティに関する市民意識の違いも見てとれる。損保ジャパンが国内で実施したSDGsに関する市民アンケート結果をみると，SDGsの認知度や環境意識は決して低くないが，政治的リーダーシップやESG投資といった，政治・経済の力を用いた変革の関心よりも，マイバッグの持参など，自分の身のまわりの日常行動への意識の方が強いことがうかがえる[9]。

一人ひとりの地道な行動の積み重ねも，もちろん重要である。しかし，残念ながらその積み重ねだけでは真の解決にはならない。今SDGsの時代に必要なのは，社会・経済をトランスフォームするような大きな変容であり，バックキャスティングで目標設定し，必要なら社会の仕組みやルールまでを変えていくことである。そうした長期視点での大きな変化を政府や企業に求める，市民一人ひとりの意識と行動こそが重要なのである。

その意味で市民の行動を促す興味深いツールがある。WBCSD（持続可能な発展のための世界経済人会議）ほかの団体が作成した，グッドライフ目標（Good Life Goals）と名付けられた，市民がSDGsの各目標達成のためにどう行動したらよいか，というヒント集である。ここでは，そうしたトランスフォーメーションを要求

する個人のアクションを推奨している。

　グッドライフ目標には，17 の目標ごとにそれぞれ 5 つの推奨アクションが書かれている。そのうちアクションの 1 から 3 までは，「気候変動の対策について学ぼう」「できる限りエネルギーを節約しよう」など，自分自身の身のまわりの行動について書かれている。しかし，4 と 5 は，「気候変動に対して大胆なアクションを今すぐ起こすよう指導者に要求しよう」「すべての人が清潔な水とトイレを使う権利を守るよう要求しよう」といった，大きな変革のために政治家などに対して要求の声をあげるべきことが書かれている。SDGs の達成には，目標 4「教育」のターゲット 4.7 に明記されたように，達成に向けて取り組む人を育むこと，つまり「持続可能な発展のための教育（ESD）」が欠かせない。そして教育においては，このように大きな変革を求めて意思表示をしたり，周囲に働きかける態度を育むことがますます必要になってきている。

　これは実は企業経営においても然りである。会社を自分の手で変えよう，と考えて行動する社員が増えることが，その企業の未来を切り開く。経済同友会の SDGs 研究会報告書[10]もその点を指摘する。報告書では経営者の視点から，社員一人ひとりが経営マインドを持って主体的に価値創造に取り組む組織をつくるうえで，SDGs は有効活用できるツールだと捉えている。全員参加型で，SDGs（社会課題）と事業（ソリューション）とを結びつけて考え企業と社会との関係を見つめなおすことが，一人ひとりの社員の貴重な教育機会となり，社員のモチベーションを高めて組織を活性化させ，変革を導く。SDGs が社員を変え，会社を変える，これは経営目線での貴重な気づきである。

　サステナブルビジネスに求められる教育は，本稿では紙数の関係で言及できなかった投資家教育[11]も含め，企業人の教育だけではなく，社会全体でのサステナビリティ主流化のための教育の一環として検討する必要がある。SDGsはそのためのよいきっかけであり，求められている社会のトランスフォーメーションのために，現在の教育のどこをどう変えなければならないのか，さまざまな角度から見直す良い機会とすべきであろう。

(1)　出所：経団連企業行動憲章（2017 年 11 月 8 日第 5 回改訂版）ちなみに改定前の憲章のサブタイトルは，「社会の信頼と共感のために」であった。

(2)　出所："SDG INDEX AND DASHBOARDS REPORT 2018 GLOBAL RESPONSIBILITIES" Bertelsmann Stiftung and Sustainable Development Solutions Network, 2018.

(3)　出所："Global Innovation Index 2019" Cornell University, INSEAD, WIPO. 対象は 129 か国・地域。

(4)　CBCC（企業市民協議会。経団連が設立したCSR の推進団体）の訪欧 CSR 対話ミッションで訪問した，スウェーデン政府（企業・イノベーション省）のプレゼンテーションから（2019 年 11 月 19 日）。

(5)　JFBS（企業と社会フォーラム）の第 9 回年次大会における，Sustainability Leadership Training のセッションでの殷格非氏のプレゼンテーションから（2019 年 9 月 6 日）。

(6)　GIZ は，毎年 6 月に北京で開催される CSR の国際フォーラムのスポンサーとして支援を続けてきた。ちなみに，この国際フォーラムには，経団連CBCC（企業市民協議会）も長年にわたり共催者として参加している。

(7)　ヨーラン・スバネリッド著・鈴木賢志編訳（2016）『スウェーデンの小学校社会科の教科書を読む：日本の大学生は何を感じたのか』新評論。

(8)　アーネ・リンドクウィスト，ヤン・ウェステル著・川上邦夫訳（1997）『あなた自身の社会―スウェーデンの中学教科書』新評論。

(9)　損害保険ジャパン日本興亜株式会社「社会的課題・SDGs に関する意識調査」2019 年 8 月。例えば，日ごろ行っている行動として，買い物時にマイバッグ持参は 68.1%，投資における ESG 考慮は5.9% など。

(10)　公益社団法人経済同友会「企業と人間社会の持続的成長のための SDGs ～価値創造に向けて，一

人ひとりが自ら考え，取り組む組織へ〜」（2019 年
7 月）。

(11)　例えば，シンガポール証券取引所では上場企業
　　に ESG 情報公開を義務付けた際に，その情報をど
　　う投資に活用したらよいかを学ぶ，機関投資家向
　　けの教育にも力を入れた。企業が苦労して開示し
　　た情報も，正しく，有効に活用されなければ意味
　　がない。こうした投資家向けの教育は重要である。

〈参考文献〉

Bertelsmann Stiftung and Sustainable Development Solutions Network (2018) *SDG Index and Dashboards Report 2018: Global Responsibilities*, Available at https://s3.amazonaws.com/sustainabledevelopment.report/2018/2018_sdg_index_and_dashboards_report.pdf, Accessed March 10th 2020.

Cornell University, INSEAD, and the World Intellectual Property Organization (2019) *Global Innovation Index 2019*, Available at https://www.wipo.int/edocs/pubdocs/en/wipo_pub_gii_2019.pdf, Accessed March 10th 2020.

United Nations (2015) *Transforming our World: 2030 agenda for Sustainable Development (A/70/L. 1)*, Available at https://www.un.org/ga/search/view_doc.asp?symbol=A/70/L.1, Accessed March 10th 2020.

アーネ・リンドクウィスト，ヤン・ウェステル著・川上邦夫訳（1997）『あなた自身の社会—スウェーデンの中学教科書』新評論。

経済同友会（2019）「企業と人間社会の持続的成長のための SDGs 〜価値創造に向けて，一人ひとりが自ら考え，取り組む組織へ〜」，Available at https://www.doyukai.or.jp/policyproposals/articles/2019/190731a.html, Accessed March 10th 2020.

日本経済団体連合会（2017a）「企業行動憲章」（2017 年11 月 8 日 第 5 回 改 訂 版），Available at https://www.keidanren.or.jp/policy/cgcb/charter2017.html, Accessed March 10th 2020.

——（2017b）「企業行動憲章実行の手引き」（2017 年11 月 8 日 第 7 回 改 訂 版），Available at https://www.keidanren.or.jp/policy/cgcb/tebiki7.html, Accessed March 10th 2020.

ヨーラン・スバネリッド著・鈴木賢志編訳（2016）『スウェーデンの小学校社会科の教科書を読む：日本の大学生は何を感じたのか』新評論。

42   Japan Forum of Business and Society Annals, No.9. pp. 42–58, 2020

The Prestige Effects of Sponsorship on Attitudes toward Corporate Brands and Art Events

Yasushi Sonobe
Professor, Faculty of Sociology, Toyo University

Makiko Kawakita
Professor, Faculty of Business Administration, Nanzan University

Key words : corporate brand, art event, sponsorship, music, art's spillover effects, perceived prestige, attitude, cultural capital, covariance structure analysis, multi-group structural equation modeling

【Abstract】

The purpose of this research is to clarify the mechanism by which corporate brands and art events bring together the images of both and promote psychological changes among consumers. Study 1 identified a process through which the perceived prestige of corporate brands and art events enhances the perceived prestige of sponsorship and, furthermore, improves attitudes toward brand and art event through attitudes toward sponsorship. Study 2 focused on opportunities to be in touch with books, music, and art as moderation valuables of the cultural capital that the stakeholder has in capturing the process. The analysis has found that although it is weak at the 0.1 level, the influence of the perceived prestige of art event on the perceived prestige of sponsorship is stronger in the high cultural capital group than in the low cultural capital group. In contrast, attitudes toward sponsorship exert a stronger influence on attitudes toward art event in the low cultural capital group than in the high cultural capital group.

1. | Introduction

Firms have long sponsored art. Art can be divided into highbrow and lowbrow art (Holbrook, 1999). For example, the German fashion brand HUGO BOSS sponsors the Solomon R. Guggenheim Museum and Foundation. It is no secret that corporations and luxury brands play an increasingly important role in funding artworks, artists, and institutions in all corners of the art world (Forbes, 2015). Companies support art in Japan too. They provide two types of art support.

Reviewed Article (Received January 28th 2020/Accepted June 2nd 2020)

First, companies support high-prestige art. In 2019, Toyota Motor Corporation sponsored the Vienna Premium Concert in six cities in Japan. The concert is composed of 30 members, including members of the Vienna State Opera and the Vienna Philharmonic, as well as artists active in Europe. It also features a few elite chamber orchestras with world-class performing technique (Toyota, 2018).

Second, high-prestige companies support artists who are expected to grow in the future. Shiseido, a cosmetics manufacture, operates the Shiseido Gallery, which is said to be the oldest existing art gallery in Japan. In the 1990s, the gallery shifted its emphasis to contemporary art and began a dynamic program aimed at introducing the expression of that era, noted for combining vanguard contemporaneity with a sense of simple purity (Shiseido Gallery website).

Holbrook (1999) pointed out that the cultural hierarchy including art is polarized and that there is a hierarchical relationship such as highbrow and lowbrow art and entertainment. The former tends to be elegant and to be practiced by non-profit organizations. The latter can be vulgar and be practiced by for-profit organizations (Yamada, 2008). When support for art is seen from the perspective of marketing, art is often included in the subjects of sponsorship as well as sports and entertainment. Sponsorship refers to investment into causes and events, which are carried out in order to support the goals of any firm or marketing agency (Gardner and Shuman, 1988).

When the promotional aspect of highbrow art becomes too explicit, it can invite criticism from the art world. For example, in Japan, from the latter half of the 1980s to the beginning of the 1990s, when support for art became mainstream, there was a backlash against its commercialization by corporations. According to Kato (2018), there was a conflict between employees who did not like the idea of using the profit they earned with their hard work to support art and those in the field of art and culture who believed that their "excellent art" should be understood by anyone.

Due to the conflict between economy and culture and firms' worsening performance, according to a survey conducted by Keidanren (*Japan Business Federation*) and One Percent Club among their corporate members, the ratio of expenditure on art support to the firms' total expenditure on contribution to society decreased from 20.8% (30.2 billion yen; N=367) in 1995 to 10.7% (18.6 billion yen; N=360) in 2013 (One Percent Club, Keidanren, 2010; 2014)[1].

However, in recent years, firms tend to be again expecting to improve their image by achieving prestige by means of support for art or corporate patronage of art (One Percent Club, Keidanren, 2018). In 2016, "the proportion of support for culture/art" came second in a list of 14 items at 17.2% (35.2 billion yen; N=343) (One Percent Club, Keidanren, 2017)[2]. According to the Association for Corporate Support for the Arts of Japan (2019), music (36.9%, N=519) and visual arts (23.8%, N=334) attract significant support from Japanese firms. The aim of corporate patronage of art is to improve the firm's image and to build a relationship with customers (Association for Corporate Support of the Arts, 2019).

Firms, because they are profit-pursuing bodies, have to be accountable to the stakeholders such as shareholders and need to explain why support for art is necessary. However, excessive reliance on support of art for marketing and sales could invite a backlash from people in the field of art. Consequently, there is a need to explain why support of art is provided as part of firms' activities. However, practitioners have not been able to show their outcome in concrete figures as business results.

Support for art can be seen as a type of sponsorship. For companies, sponsorship has the effect of advertising to consumers. There are many studies on sponsorship, particularly in reference to sports. In the field of sports, criticism against firms' support for sports in the form of sponsorships is rare. On the other hand, using support of art as a marketing tool leads to skepticism. Is it bad for art organizations that firms use the support of art in marketing? We think that even the supported arts are likely to incur the same positive effects as firms do.

The purpose of this research is to clarify the mechanism by which corporate brands and art events bring together the images of both and promote psychological changes among consumers. In particular, we aim to examine the perceived prestige effects of sponsorship for arts on consumer attitudes to corporate brands and art events. In addition, we also examine how the degree to which consumers themselves were exposed to cultural influences, such as a tradition of music and art in the family, affects these causal rela-

tionships.

2. | A review of preceding studies

Research on corporate art support can be divided into three areas: Patronage (*mécénat*) as corporate philanthropy, sponsorship in advertising, and image transfer of art in consumer behavior. We will review each of these.

2-1. *Mécénat*

In Japan, art support from the private sector began around the 17th century, when the Edo period started. Wealthy merchants developed various cultures such as Ukiyo-e, Kabuki, and crafts, which in turn spread as townsman culture. For example, the Mitsui family (later Mitsui Zaibatsu) were not only rich merchants but also patrons of art (Tsuji, 2005; Hayashi, 2004). When the isolation policy ended and the Meiji era began, Japan adopted Western culture. The wealthy merchants formed a conglomerate, and their founders enthusiastically introduced their art collections into Japan.

According to Hayashi (2004), Kojiro Matsukata eagerly collected French art and laid the foundation for later Western art collections. Magosaburo Ohara introduced Western paintings to Japan with the support of the painter Torajiro Kojima and established the Ohara Museum of Art, which is still a regional resource (Hayashi, 2004). During this period, many companies tried to establish their own corporate brands by promoting culture. Since the Meiji era, Shiseido, a major cosmetics manufacturer, has regarded culture as an asset. It owns a gallery with many in-house artists to disseminate its culture.

According to Kawashima (2012), different businesses became involved with art and culture after World War II, particularly during the 1970s and 1980s, a period of economic development, with the gross national product growing at more than 10% annually. For example, the Saison Group, a retail business, property development, and finance conglomerate, promoted culture through museums and publishing companies as the driver of consumption, emphasizing lifestyle as the basis of the spirit of the times in department stores (Kawashima, 2012).

Since the 1970s, various corporate foundations that support art have been established. With the establishment of the Association for Corporate Support of the Arts in 1990, *mécénat* and social contributions became popular. Kawashima (2012) characterizes art support by companies in Japan as follows. In the absence of an official cultural policy and experts to manage art, Japanese companies provide their own art support. In the process, corporate involvement with the arts and culture in Japan has broken fresh ground, taking a route between commercial sponsorship and corporate philanthropy (Kawashima, 2012).

2-2. Sponsorship

Little research has been done on sponsorship and philanthropy in the arts sector, particularly with regard to consumer behavior (Walliser, 2003; Colbert, d'Astous and Parmentier, 2005). In fact, the authors have investigated the research trends since 2000 using EBSCO, a paper search service. According to the

search results, 7 peer-reviewed papers included "art and sponsorship" in the title, whereas "sports and sponsorship" occurred in 37 paper titles.

Therefore, we argue that sponsorship research is far less relevant to art than sports. Several studies have examined the impact of sponsorship on consumer perception (d'Astous and Bitz, 1995; Colbert et al., 2005; Carrillat and d'Astous, 2012; Woisetschläger and Michaelis, 2012). However, much of the research is about sports sponsorship.

Colbert et al. (2005) divided art sponsorship into several types and produced fictional articles by type. Then, they presented them to consumers and investigated the extent to which they liked the articles. Colbert et al. (2005) used the following variables for art sponsorship programs: three types of sponsors (government ministries, Crown corporation, private companies), nature of sponsorship (philanthropic or commercial), perceived congruence between the sponsor and the sponsored event, the form of the cultural events (high art versus popular art and performing arts versus heritage arts). For an overall evaluation of the sponsorship program, they adopted perception as the dependent variable. The analysis revealed significant differences depending on the type of sponsorship.

Despite sponsorship studies with an advertising perspective, very few have focused on the consumer's perception. Colbert et al. (2005) deal with art but focus on cultural policy. Therefore, their concept of consumer perception is not exact and includes the attitude that results from perception. However, perception and attitude are different concepts in the context of consumer behavior.

2-3. Image transfer of brand and art

According to the American Marketing Association, a brand is a name, term, design, symbol, or any other feature that identifies one seller's good or service as distinct from those of other sellers (MASB: Marketing Accountability Standards Board, 2019). A brand is a general concept used to describe products, but it can be applied to a certain organization or group like a corporate brand.

The functions of a corporate brand include conveying the corporation's value, providing the means to differentiate the product from the competitors' products, and improving the stakeholders' evaluation of and loyalty toward the organization (Balmer and Gray, 2003). Corporate brands include company names such as Toyota Motor Corporation, departments that produce high-end brands such as Lexus, and group companies such as Daihatsu, which mainly manufactures light cars at Toyota Motor Corporation's subsidiaries.

Whether it is about a corporate brand or a product brand, consumers perceive brand knowledge. According to Keller (2003), consumer brand knowledge can be defined in terms of the personal meaning of a brand stored in the consumer's memory, that is, all descriptive and evaluative brand-related information. Brand knowledge is not limited to knowledge about the brand itself, but it can also include information from secondary sources outside the firm. Secondary sources that enhance brand knowledge include various means such as the other brand, people, places, and things (one of the aspects of "things" being events) (Keller, 2003). Support for art is included in events, and firms can extend the brand association of the firm by enlisting the help of the art event that the firm supports.

Some of the images attached to the brand are based on prestige (Park, Milberg, and Lawson, 1991). According to Vigneron and Johnson (1999) perceived prestige is seen as a signal of status and wealth in the brand, and the higher the price is, the more valuable the brand becomes, satisfying emotional needs. Luxury brands that deal with automobiles, cosmetics, and fashion have a strong tendency to perceive prestige.

Prestige can also be perceived from art related to a product purchase or consumption. According to Hagtvedt and Patrick (2008), art is considered to have spillover effects. Spillover effects have been found regarding music in the store (Gorn, 1982) or a fragrance (Spangenberg, Crowley, and Henderson, 1996) when purchasing a product, and they can be applied to visual art (Hagtvedt and Patrick, 2008).

2-4. Review summery

In this section, we organize existing research on corporate art support into three areas: *mécénat*, sponsorship, and image transfer of brand and art. Subsection 2.1 (*Mécénat*) show the Japanese private sector provides art support.

Around the 17th century, when *mécénat* began in earnest in Japan, it was the wealthy individuals who mainly supported the arts, but in the latter half of the 20th century, major corporations achieved economic growth and became the center of art support. Kawashima (2012) pointed out that corporate art support has taken root in Japanese society, with a vague difference between *mécénat* as philanthropy and sponsorship to enhance brand value.

Reviewing the research on sponsorship, we found a few recent studies on art support, most of them on sports. In addition, some studies focus on consumer perception, but they have some limitations, such as confusion regarding psychological causal relationships between consumers, perception, and attitude, typical in consumer behavior research.

In this research, we focus on the fact that both corporate brands and art events have prestige, which has a psychological effect on the consumers who perceive it. Brands can form images from a variety of secondary factors, including art events. Thus, we assume the following. Art is associated with prestige, which can be transferred to corporate brands through sponsorship. On the other hand, corporate brands, especially high-end brands, have prestige themselves, which can be transferred to art events supported by companies.

Most sponsorship research is about sports, so there is a lack of focus on prestige, which is inherent in both corporate brands and art events. Research on the prestige of corporate brands and art events can be found in the area of spillover effects. Therefore, we will build a model in the next section to examine how consumers perceive the prestige of corporate brands and art events through the sponsorship that companies provide and what

psychological effect the perceived prestige has on customers.

3. | Framework

As mentioned earlier, prestige is included in brand image (Park, Milberg and Lawson, 1991), and is especially perceived in luxury brands (Vigneron and Johnson, 1999). This is primarily related to product brands, but it can also be applied to corporate brands. On the other hand, spillover effects cause people to perceive prestige from art (Hagtvedt and Patrick, 2008). When a company sponsors an arts event, the sponsorship itself can have a perceptual prestige due to the combination of the corporate brand and the arts event.

An example is the Vienna Premium Concert sponsored by Toyota Motor and Shiseido Gallery, introduced at the beginning of this article. In addition, an apparel company sponsored the "UNIQLO Free Friday Night" program. The program began in 2013 with free admission to the Museum of Modern Art (MoMA) every Friday afternoon and evening (UNIQLO, 2019). Combining these examples with the above theory, we propose the following hypothesis.

H1a Perceived prestige of a corporate brand would exert a positive influence on perceived prestige of sponsorship.

H1b Perceived prestige of an art event would exert a positive influence on perceived prestige of sponsorship.

One of the outcome indicators of spillover effects is attitude. Attitude is defined as the learned belief, senses, and tendency in a response (Sternthal and Craig, 1982), and is related to the evaluation an individual makes about whether he/she likes it, or the behavior in question (Ajzen and Fishbein, 1977; Ajzen, 1991). Concrete indicators include like/dislike, desirability, goodness, and so on (Osgood, Suci, and Tannenbaum, 1957; Simonin and Ruth, 1998).

Hagtvedt and Patrick (2008) have demonstrated that art has spillover effects on consumer goods. They conducted a questionnaire survey with consumers by presenting them with products that had works of art printed on them on a smaller scale. The result has shown that a work of art displayed on a product enhanced its perceived prestige and improved the attitude toward the product (Hagtvedt and Patrick, 2008). In addition, Lee, Chen, and Wang (2014) have shown that in a luxury brand, perceived prestige is enhanced for products with artwork than those without it.

These findings suggest that when a firm supports the activities of art organizations as a sponsor, it is likely that the consumer would perceive prestige in the sponsorship, which combines both firms and activities of art organizations. Additionally, as the artistic prestige that is attached to a product improves the consumer's product attitude (Hagtvedt and Patrick, 2008), we predict that the prestige of sponsorship would exert an influence on the attitude toward sponsorship. Furthermore, attitudes toward sponsorship would exert some influence on attitudes toward the corporate brand as well as on the art event in which there is a collaboration in the form of a spon-

sorship. In other words, assuming that perceived prestige, which is one of the factors of spillover effects, affects attitudes as outcome indicators of these effects, we propose the following hypotheses:

> H2　Perceived prestige of a sponsorship would exert a positive influence on attitudes toward sponsorship.
>
> H3a　Attitudes toward sponsorship would exert a positive influence on attitudes toward a corporate brand.
>
> H3b　Attitudes toward sponsorship would exert a positive influence on attitudes toward an art event.

On the other hand, we can assume that consumers' cultural capital would exert its influence as a moderator on the relationship between the concepts described above. According to Bourdieu (1986), cultural capital is made up of the following three states: first, the embodied state as the permanent nature of the mind and body; second, the objectified state such as paintings, books, dictionaries, tools, and machines, and; third, the institutionalized state.

To improve one's embodied state, the family environment in which one grows up, in other words, the degree to which one is surrounded by authentic culture (books, music, art and other cultural expressions), is important (Flemmen, Jarness, and Rosenlund, 2017). This suggests that contact with culture while growing up would further enhance the processes from the prestige of art to the prestige of sponsorship, to the attitude toward spon-

Figure 1   Framework

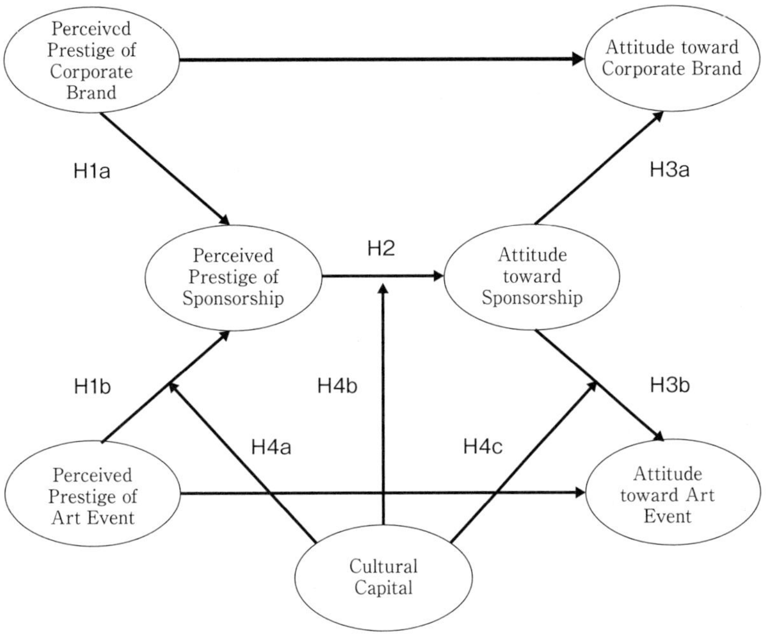

sorship, and also from the attitude toward sponsorship to the attitude toward the art event. Based on these, we propose the following hypotheses:

H4a   Cultural capital would positively enhance the influence exerted by the prestige of art on the perceived prestige of sponsorship.

H4b   Cultural capital would positively enhance the influence exerted by the perceived prestige of sponsorship on the attitude toward sponsorship.

H4c   Cultural capital would positively enhance the influence exerted by the attitude toward sponsorship on the attitude toward an art event.

Figure 1 shows the framework composed of all hypotheses that we have proposed. The next section describes the research and analysis carried out to test the proposed framework.

4.　Research and analysis

4-1. Study 1

We conducted an Internet-based survey using panel data held by My Voice Communications Inc., a research company. First, we created two sponsorships by combining corporate brands (automobile manufacturers: Lexus/Daihatsu) and the art event supported by them (Vienna Philharmonic Orchestra/ Disney On Ice). Then, we presented these combinations to four groups that were divided evenly in terms of age and gender.

In order to test H1a, H1b, H2, H3a, and H3b, we asked the respondents to answer the questions about observed variables related to

Table 1　Factor analysis (perceived prestige and attitude)

Item	Factors					
	F1	F2	F3	F4	F5	F6
Luxurious in Sponsorship	**.98**	.01	−.01	.00	.00	−.05
Prestigious in Sponsorship	**.96**	.01	.00	.00	.01	−.01
High class in Sponsorship	**.94**	.03	.02	−.02	.01	.00
Luxurious in Art Event	.05	**.84**	.00	.02	−.03	.04
Prestigious in Art Event	−.01	**.96**	−.02	.01	.03	.00
High class in Art Event	.01	**.94**	.02	.01	.00	−.03
Positive to Corporate Brand	.01	−.02	**.96**	.02	−.02	−.05
Favorable to Corporate Brand	.01	−.03	**.94**	.02	−.01	.02
Good to Corporate Brand	−.01	.05	**.90**	−.01	.03	.01
Positive to Art Event	.00	−.03	.02	**.95**	.01	−.03
Favorable to Art Event	.02	.03	.01	**.93**	−.01	−.01
Good to Art Event	.01	.06	.01	**.87**	.01	.03
Luxurious in Corporate Brand	.01	−.03	−.07	.03	**.94**	−.04
Prestigious in Corporate Brand	.01	.05	.11	−.02	**.76**	.07
High class in Corporate Brand	−.01	−.01	−.01	−.01	**.997**	−.01
Positive to Sponsorship	.40	−.07	.02	.11	−.02	**.52**
Favorable to Sponsorship	.25	.00	−.01	−.01	.01	**.78**
Good to Sponsorship	.21	.06	.00	.04	.00	**.70**
Eigenvalue	9.92	2.15	1.41	1.17	.78	.34
Factor contribution ratio	55.13	11.95	7.84	6.50	4.32	1.89
Accumulation factor contribution ratio	55.13	67.08	74.92	81.42	85.74	87.63
Cronbach's α	.97	.95	.96	.96	.97	.95

F1：Perceived Prestige of Sponsorship, F2：Perceived Prestige of Art Event, F3：Attitude toward Corporate Brand, F4：Attitude toward Art Event, F5：Perceived Prestige of Corporate Brand, F6：Attitude toward Sponsorship, Factor extraction method: principal factor method, rotation: Kaiser normalized Promax rotation; figures in bold: factor loading of adopted factors

each latent variable. The items for perceived prestige (luxurious, prestigious, and high class) we used are from Hagtvedt and Patrick (2008), and the items of attitude (positive and favorable) are those of Osgood et al. (1957) and Simonin and Ruth (1998). We asked the respondents to use a five-point Likert scale: "1. Not applicable at all", "2. Not very applicable", "3. Neither", "4. Rather applicable" and "5. Very applicable" (Please refer to the appendix for details of the questionnaire).

We collected the data as follows. We conducted a pre-test with 160 Japanese consumers aged between 20 and 59 from April 23 to 25, 2019. After analyzing the obtained data, we revised some questionnaire items. We con-

ducted the main survey with 1,024 Japanese consumers aged between 20 and 59 from May 15 to 19, 2019. Data collection was kept open until the set number of valid responses was achieved. We used IBM SPSS Statistics to produce descriptive statistics and to conduct a factor analysis. IBM SPSS Amos was used for covariance structure analysis and multigroup analysis.

Williams, Onsman, and Brown (2010) describe two major classes of factor analysis: exploratory factor analysis (EFA) and confirmatory factor analysis (CFA). EFA has been one of the most widely used statistical procedures in psychological research (Fabrigar, Wegener, MacCallum and Strahan 1999). It allows the re-

Figure 2   All samples

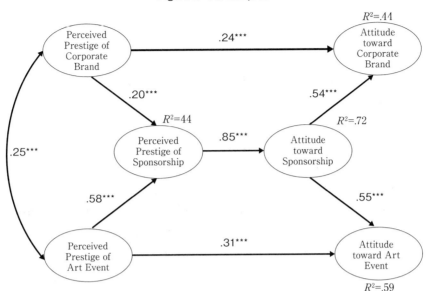

N=1,024, Standardization factor, *** p<.001

searcher to explore the main dimensions to generate a theory or model from a relatively large set of latent constructs, often represented by a set of items. However, the researcher uses CFA to test a proposed theory (Williams et al., 2010). Although the framework in this study combines existing theories, we used EFA to examine the validity of the constituent concepts of data because they had not yet been confirmed.

For the factor extraction, we applied the principal factor method and set the number of factors to 6 based on preceding studies. This found a correlation among factors. Consequently, a Kaiser normalized Promax rotation was applied. The result shows that the eigenvalue was .31, the cumulative contribution ratio was 87.62, and six factors were extracted (Table 1). The internal consistency of each factor turned out to be: a =.97 for F1, a =.96 for

F2, a =.95 for F3, a =.96 for F4, a =.93 for F5, and a =.95 for F6.

We follow the broad consensus that $.80 \leq a$ $< .90$ is evaluated as good. Consequently, we conducted a covariance structure analysis with all factors intact. Based on the proposed framework, we constructed an initial model. This model consists of all observed variables: Perceived Prestige of Corporate Brand, Perceived Prestige of Art, Perceived Prestige of Sponsorship, Attitude toward Sponsorship, Attitude toward Corporate Brand, and Attitude toward Art Event. Then, we analyzed this model.

Following a procedure to achieve path coefficients with significance of less than 5%, most often applied in psychology, we adopted the model shown in Figure 2. The goodness-of-fit of the model was: χ^2=797.93, p=.00, GFI=.92, AGFI=.89, CFI=.97, RMR=.08, and RM-

SEA=.07. The confirmation of the square of the multiple correlation coefficient (i.e., the coefficient of determination) turned out to be: R^2=.44 for Perceived Prestige of Sponsorship, R^2=.72 for Attitude toward Sponsorship, R^2=.42 for Attitude toward Corporate Brand, and R^2=.59 for Attitude toward Art Event.

As for the path coefficient, the influence of Perceived Prestige of Corporate Brand on Perceived Prestige of Sponsorship was γ=.20 (standardized coefficient, hereafter the same) and the influence of Perceived Prestige of Art Event to Perceived Prestige of Sponsorship was γ=.58 (p<.001). Next, the influence of Perceived Prestige of Sponsorship on Attitude toward Sponsorship was γ=.85 (p<.001), which was strong. The influence of Attitude toward Sponsorship on Attitude toward Corporate Brand was γ=.54 (p<.001), and that of Attitude toward Sponsorship on Attitude toward Art Event was γ=.55 (p<.001). Therefore, H1a, H1b, H2, H3a, and H3b were supported.

4-2. Study 2

Next, in order to test H4a, H4b, and H4c, we divided the sample into two groups according to the volume of cultural capital, and conducted amulti-group structural equation modeling. As for the observed variables of cultural capital, based on a scale used by Flemmen et al. (2017) to measure art in cultural capital, we adopted three items: books, classical music, and art. We asked the participants to respond to the question "Did you have many opportunities to be in contact with the following in the family in which you grew up?" for each of the three items on a four-point Likert scale of

Table 2　Factor analysis (cultural capital)

Item	Factor
Books	.57
Classical Music	.82
Art	.81
Eigenvalue	1.65
Factor contribution ratio	54.89
Cronbach's a	.77

"1. Not applicable at all", "2. Not very applicable", "3. Rather applicable" and "4. Very applicable."

We conducted a factor analysis with the principal factor method and Promax rotation with responses to the three items of cultural capital, and the analysis yielded one factor (Table 2). Its internal consistency was a=.77. We follow the broad consensus that $.70 \leq a < .80$ is acceptable. Consequently, in the current study, we used all observed variables for the analysis.

We used the principal component analysis to synthesize the three variables. The results produced a mean of 0 with a variance of 1. Accordingly, those participants whose figures were larger than 0 were classified as a high cultural capital group (N=461) and those with figures smaller than 0 were classified as a low cultural capital group (N=563). We tested the hypotheses by applying multi-group structural equation modeling to these two groups. In this analysis, the procedure to adopt paths with less than 5% significance was used as in Study 1, and the model shown in Figure 3 was adopted. The goodness-of-fit of the model was χ^2=1036.92, p=.00, GFI=.90, AGFI=.86, CFI=.97, RMR=.08, RMSEA=.06 (Figure 3).

Let us now examine the path coefficients related to the hypotheses. As for the influence

Figure 3   Multigroup analysis (cultural capital)

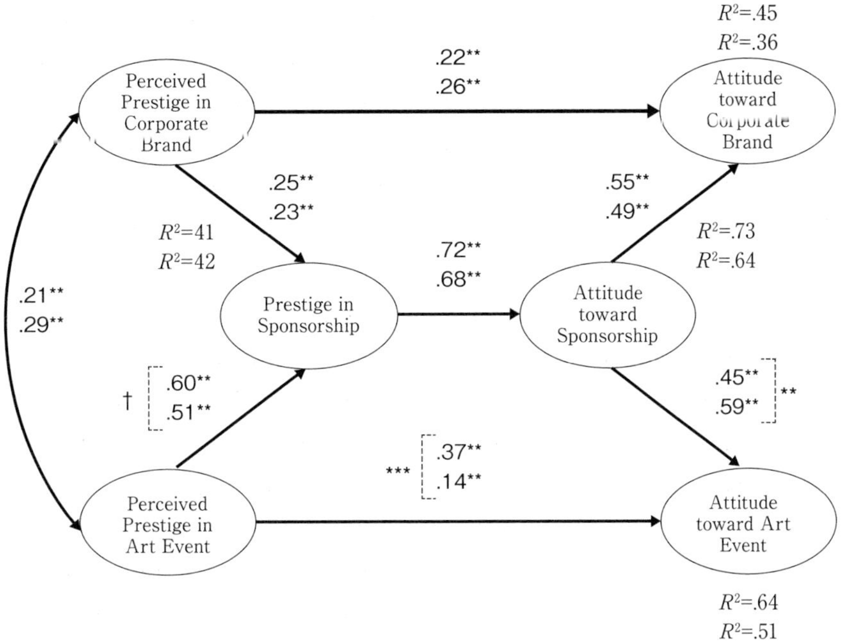

Upper row: High Group (N=461), Lower row: Low Group (N=563), Non-standardization factor,
*** p<.001, ** p<.01, † p<.10

of Perceived Prestige of Art Event on Perceived Prestige of Sponsorship, it was γ =.60 for the high cultural capital group and γ =.51 for the low cultural capital group. The test statistic for the difference between the non-standardization factors of both coefficients was D=|1.75| (p<.10). As a result, H4a is only partially supported. As for the influence of Perceived Prestige of Sponsorship on Attitude toward Sponsorship, it was γ =.72 for the high cultural capital group and γ =.68 for the low cultural capital group. The test statistic for the difference between the two was D=|.88| (p>.10). Therefore, H4b was rejected.

Lastly, as for the influence of Attitude toward Sponsorship on Attitude toward Art Event, it was γ =.45 for the high cultural capital group and γ =.59 for the low cultural capi-

tal group, which suggests a larger influence for the low cultural capital group. The test statistic for the difference between the two was D=|2.52| (p<.05). Therefore, H4c was rejected. In addition, although this was not considered a hypothesis, a significant difference was found in the path from Perceived Prestige of Art Event to Attitude toward Art Event, and the high cultural capital group showed a larger value (γ =.37) than the low cultural capital group (γ =.14). The test statistic for the difference between the parameters was D=|5.46| (p<.001). No other path was significantly influenced by the volume of cultural capital.

5. | Discussion

The preceding analyses yielded the following results. Study 1 identified a process through which the perceived prestige of corporate brands and art events enhances the perceived prestige of sponsorship and furthermore, improves attitudes toward brand and art event through attitudes toward sponsorship.

Study 2 focused on opportunities to be in touch with books, music, and art as moderation valuables of the cultural capital that the stakeholder has in capturing the process. The analysis has found that although it is weak at the 0.1 level, the influence of the perceived prestige of art event on the perceived prestige of sponsorship is stronger in the high cultural capital group than in the low cultural capital group. In addition, the perceived prestige of art event exerts a direct influence on the attitude toward art events, which is stronger in the high cultural capital group than in the low cultural capital group.

In contrast, attitudes toward sponsorship exert a stronger influence on attitudes toward art event in the low cultural capital group than in the high cultural capital group. While the high cultural capital group places more emphasis on the perceived prestige of art event, the low cultural capital group emphasizes the attitude toward sponsorship. In other words, this research suggests that a high level of cultural capital strengthens the influence of the perceived prestige of art event, but weakens the influence of the attitude toward sponsorship.

The current study's academic and practical contributions are as follows. In terms of academic contribution, the study has captured a psychological effect of art sponsorship on the perceived prestige and attitude in the field of sponsorship studies, which is dominated by sports. Although the spillover effects of the perceived prestige of art events have been discussed in other studies, the discussion was limited to experiments on artwork attached to the product's package or the product itself.

In contrast, the current study focused on how art events supported by firms influence the evaluation of corporate brands or the art events themselves. Furthermore, no study has identified the process through which the perceived prestige of art event and corporate brand improves attitudes toward art and toward the corporate brand, through sponsorship.

The practical contribution has two categories: firms that support art and art organizations that receive support. First, the contribution to firms is as follows. The current study suggests that a firm can improve attitudes toward its own brand through sponsorship by focusing on the perceived prestige of corporate brands and art events.

In addition, the study suggests that the perceived prestige of art events exerts a stronger influence on the perceived prestige of sponsorships than on the perceived prestige of corporate brands. This shows that firms can improve attitudes toward their own brand by supporting art events and benefiting from the prestige attached to them. These findings should be suggestive for firms that are accountable to stakeholders, such as shareholders, in regard to their activities to support art.

Next, the contribution to art organizations is as follows. As mentioned at the beginning, art organizations are concerned that firms would take advantage of their activities to promote their corporate brand. However, the current study found that support for an art event brings with it non-financial benefits to the art organization: attitude toward art events improves with firms' support to art organizations.

Additionally, the study found the influence of cultural capital on variables related to art only. Perceived prestige has a stronger effect in the high cultural capital group than in the low cultural capital group. However, the influence of attitudes toward sponsorship on attitudes toward art events is stronger in the low cultural capital group than in the high cultural capital group. This suggests the importance, for both firms and art organizations that engage with low cultural capital groups, of promoting sponsorships through appropriate communication programs, such as a campaign to build familiarity with their sponsorships, rather than pursuing perceived prestige.

While the current study has made the contributions described above, there are some challenges left. While the samples we use in this study are standardized for gender and age, the total number of observations is 1,024, which is not very large. This implies the need to take even more accurate measurements using a larger sample. Also, the analyses in the study have not shed enough light on the relationship between the combinations of corporate brands and the support of art.

Initially, we planned to compare the differences between high and low art as company support destinations. However, when the manipulation check was performed, the evaluations of the subjects were not complete. Further testing is necessary to match firms and art events considering the degree of prestige. We would like to address these challenges separately in the future.

(1) We calculated each absolute measure by multiplying the total expenditure for social philanthropic activities by the percentage of spending on culture and art. However, these amounts of money are approximate values because the number of response samples for the former and for the spending ratio by field are different. According to a survey conducted in 1995, the total expenditure for social philanthropic activities were 145.4 billion yen (N=367), and the number of respondents in the expenditure ratio by field was not disclosed (One Percent Club, Keidanren, 2010). According to a 2013 survey, expenditure on social philanthropic activities was 173.5 billion yen (N=360), and the number of respondents in the expenditure ratio by field was 350 companies (One Percent Club, Keidanren, 2014).

(2) As in Note (1), these amounts of money are approximate values because the number of response samples for the former and for the spending ratio by field are different. Spending on social philanthropic activities was 204.9 billion yen (N=343), and the number of respondents in the expenditure ratio by field was 336 companies.

This work was supported by JSPS KAKENHI under Grant Number JP 17K03903 and Nanzan University Pache Research Subsidy I-A-2 for the 2020 academic year.

〈References〉

Ajzen I. (1991) 'The theory of planned behavior', *Orga-*

nizational Behavior and Human Decision Process-es, Volume 50, No. 2, pp. 179–211.

—— and Fishbein, M. (1977) 'Attitude-behavior relations: A theoretical analysis and review of empirical research', *Psychological Bulletin*, Volume 84, No. 5, pp. 888–918.

Association for Corporate Support of the Arts (2019) *Mécénat Report 2019*, Association for Corporate Support of the Arts, Available at https://www.mécénat.or.jp/ja/wp-content/uploads/MécénatReport2019.pdf, Accessed May 1st 2020 (in Japanese).

Balmer, J.M.T. and Gray, E.R. (2003) 'Corporate brands: what are they? What of them?', *European Journal of Marketing*, Volume 37, Issue 7–8, pp. 972–997.

Bourdieu, P. (1986) 'The Forms of Capital', in J. Richardson (ed.), *Handbook of Theory and Research for the Sociology of Education*, NY: Greenwood, pp. 241–258.

Carrillat, F.A. and d'Astous, A. (2012) 'The sponsorship-advertising interface: is less better for sponsors?', *European Journal of Marketing*, Volume 46, No. 3/4, pp. 562–574.

Colbert, F., d'Astous, A. and Parmentier, M.A. (2005) 'Consumer Perceptions of Private versus Public Sponsorship of the Arts', *International Journal of Arts Management*, Volume 8, No. 1, pp. 48–59.

d'Astous, A. and Bitz, P. (1995) 'Consumer Evaluations of Sponsorship Programmes', *European Journal of Marketing*, Volume 29, No. 12, pp. 6–22.

Fabrigar, L.R., Wegener, D.T., MacCallum, R.C. and Strahan, E.J. (1999) 'Evaluating the Use of Exploratory Factor Analysis in Psychological Research', *Psychological Methods*, Volume 4, Issue 3, pp. 272–299.

Flemmen, M.P., Jerness, V. and Rosenlund, L. (2017) 'Social Space and Cultural Class Divisions: The Forms of Capital and Contemporary Lifestyle Differentiation', *British Journal of Sociology*, Volume 69, Issue 1, pp. 124–153.

Forbes, A. (2015) 'Three Basel Projects Show a New Era of Corporate Patronage', *Artsy*, Available at https://www.artsy.net/article/artsy-editorial-new-era-of-corporate-art-sponsorship, Accessed April 21st 2020.

Gardner, M.P. and Shuman, P. (1988) 'Sponsorships and Small Businesses', *Journal of Small Business Management*, Volume 26, Issue 4, pp. 44–52.

Gorn, G.J. (1982) 'The Effects of Music in Advertising on Choice Behavior: A Classical Conditioning Ap-

proach', *Journal of Marketing*, Volume 46, Issue 1, pp. 94–101.

Hagtvedt, H. and Patrick, V.M. (2008) 'Art Infusion: The Influence of Visual Art on the Perception and Evaluation of Consumer Products', *Journal of Marketing Research*, Volume 45, Issue 3, pp. 379–389.

Hayashi, Y. (2004) *Evolving Arts Management*, Leyline-Publishing (in Japanese).

Holbrook, M.B. (1999) 'Popular Appeal versus Expert Judgments of Motion Pictures', *Journal of Consumer Research*, Volume 26, Issue 2, pp. 144–155.

Kato, T. (2018) *The Investment Effect of Art and Culture: Mécénat and Creative Economy*, Suiyo-sya (in Japanese).

Kawashima, N. (2012) 'Corporate support for the Arts in Japan: Beyond Emulation of the Western Models', *International Journal of Cultural Policy*, Volume 18, Issue 3, pp. 1–13.

Keller, K.L. (2003) 'Brand Synthesis: The Multidimensionality of Brand Knowledge', *Journal of Consumer Research*, Volume 29, Issue 4, pp. 595–600.

Kries, M., *Arts Sponsorship at HUGO BOSS: A Longstanding Tradition*, Available at https://group.hugoboss.com/en/sponsorship/arts-sponsorship, Accessed April 21st 2020.

Kyodo Tokyo, *Disney On Ice*, Available at https://www.kyodotokyo.com/doi, Accessed May 2nd 2020 (in Japanese).

Lee, H.C., Chen, W.W. and Wang, C.W. (2015) 'The Role of Visual Art in Enhancing Perceived Prestige of Luxury Brands', *Marketing Letter*, Volume 26, Issue 4, pp. 593–606.

Levine, L.W. (1988) *Highbrow/Lowbrow: The Emergence of Cultural Hierarchy in America*, Boston: Harvard University Press, Tsuneyama, N. (Tr.), (2005) Keio University Press (in Japanese).

MASB: Marketing Accountability Standards Board (2019) *Common Language Marketing Dictionary*, Available at https://marketing-dictionary.org/, Accessed December 5th 2019.

One Percent Club, Keidanren (2010) *Survey Results of Social Contribution Activities in Fiscal 2009*, Available at http://www.keidanren.or.jp/policy/2010/095kekka.pdf, Accessed December 5th 2019 (in Japanese).

—— (2014) *Survey Results of Social Contribution Activities in Fiscal 2013*, Available at http://www.keidanren.or.jp/policy/2014/082_honbun.pdf, Accessed December 5th 2019 (in Japanese).

—— (2017) *Survey Results of Social Contribution Activities in Fiscal 2016*, Available at https://www.keidanren.or.jp/policy/2017/091_honbun.pdf, Accessed December 5th 2019 (in Japanese).

—— (2018) *Survey Results of Social Contribution Activities in Fiscal 2017*, Available at http://www.keidanren.or.jp/policy/2018/097_honbun.pdf, Accessed December 5th 2019 (in Japanese).

Osgood, C.E., Suci, G.J. and Tannenbaum, P.H. (1957) *The Measurement of Meaning*, University of Illinois Press, Urbana.

Park, C.W., Milberg, S. and Lawson, R. (1991) 'Evaluation of Brand Extensions: The Role of Product Feature Similarity and Brand Concept Consistency', *Journal of Consumer Research*, Volume 18, Issue 2, pp. 185-193.

Simonin, B.L. and Ruth, J.A. (1998) 'Is a Company Known by the Company It Keeps? Assessing the Spillover Effects of Brand Alliances on Consumer Brand Attitudes', *Journal of Marketing Research*, Volume 35, No. 1, pp. 30-42.

Shiseido Gallery, *Introducing the Shiseido Gallery*, Available at https://gallery.shiseido.com/en/, Accessed May 6th 2020.

Spangenberg, E.R., Crowley, A.E. and Henderson, P.W. (1996) 'Improving the Store Environment: Do Olfactory Cues Affect Evaluations and Behaviors?', *Journal of Marketing*, Volume 60, Issue 2, pp. 67-80.

Sternthal, B. and Craig, C.S. (1982) *Consumer behavior: An Information Processing Perspective*, Prentice-Hall, New Jersey.

Suntory Group (2018) *Vienna Philharmonic Week in Japan 2018 Daiwa House Special Franz Welser-Mest Conductor Vienna Philharmonic Orchestra*, Available at https://www.suntory.co.jp/news/article/sh0264.html, Accessed May 2nd 2020 (in Japanese).

Toyota (2018) *Vienna Premium Concert*, Available at https://www.toyota.co.jp/jpn/sustainability/social_contribution/society_and_culture/domestic/tomas/pdf/wpc_pamphlet.pdf, Accessed April 21st 2020 (in Japanese).

Tsuji, N. (2005) *History of Art in Japan*, University of Tokyo Press (in Japanese).

UNIQLO (2019) *"UTGP 2020 + MoMA" will be held in cooperation with MoMA, The theme for 2020 is "DRAW YOUR WORLD"*, Starting today, September 13th (Fri), worldwide, 2020 September 13th, Available at https://www.uniqlo.com/jp/corp/pressrelease/2019/09/momautgp_2020_moma_2020draw_yo.html, Accessed May 6th 2020 (in Japanese).

Vigneron, F. and Johnson, L.W. (1999) 'A Review and a Conceptual Framework of Prestige-Seeking Consumer Behavior', *Academy of Marketing Science Review*, Volume 1, pp. 1-15.

Walliser, B. (2003) 'An International Review of Sponsorship Research: Extension and Update', *International Journal of Advertising*, Volume 22, pp. 5-40.

Williams, B., Onsman, A. and Brown, T. (2010) 'Exploratory Factor Analysis: A five-Step Guide for Novices', *Journal of Emergency Primary Health Care*, Volume 8, Issue 3, pp. 1-13.

Woisetschläger, D.M. and Michaelis, M. (2012) 'Sponsorship Congruence and Brand Image: A Pre-post Event Analysis', *European Journal of Marketing*, Volume 46, No. 3/4, pp. 509-523.

Yamada, S. (2008) *Introduction to Arts Marketing: Designing Strategies for the Art Market*, Suiyo-sya (in Japanese).

Appendix: Survey questionnaire

1. Please tell us your gender.

   Proportion: Male 50%, Female 50%

2. Please tell us your age.

   Proportion: 20s 25.0%, 30s 25.0%, 40s 25.0%, 50s 25.0%

· Combination of corporate brands and art supported by them (equal allocation by age and gender)

   A Lexus × Vienna Philharmonic Orchestra "Chamber Music Special" (N=256)

   B Lexus × Feld Entertainment "Disney On Ice" (N=256)

   C Daihatsu × Feld Entertainment "Disney On Ice" (N=256)

   D Daihatsu × Vienna Philharmonic Orchestra "Chamber Music Special" (N=256)

3. Did you have many opportunities to be in contact with the following in the family in which you grew up?

   Items: Books, Classical music, Art (painting, sculpture, etc.)

   Choices: "1. Not applicable at all", "2. Not very applicable", "3. Rather applicable" and "4. Very applicable."

4. We would like to ask you about the brand called

Lexus/Daihatsu (show one or the other, the same applies below). Please give one answer for each of these brands.

Items: Luxurious, Prestigious, High class

Choices: "1. Not applicable at all", "2. Not very applicable", "3. Neither", "4. Rather applicable" and "5. Very applicable."

5. Next, I would like to ask about the Vienna Philharmonic Orchestra "Chamber Music Special" / Feld Entertainment "Disney On Ice." See the explanation below.

· Vienna Philharmonic Orchestra "Chamber Music Special"*

Founded in 1842, and with a history of 177 years, the Vienna Philharmonic Orchestra cultivates tradition in the musical capital of Vienna, which has produced famous composers and performers, and as a world-class orchestra, its unique and rich sound attracts the world's audience. For this performance in Tokyo, members of the Vienna Philharmonic Orchestra, who are familiar with operas at the Vienna State Opera, will deliver "chamber music specials" in which they "sing" operas with various instrumental arrangements.

· Feld Entertainment "Disney On Ice"**

Disney On Ice is a musical on ice that has been loved by generations of generations as one of the world's leading live entertainment provided by Feld Entertainment. In Japan, since *Happy Birthday Donald* was released in 1986, we deliver movie stories such as *Aladdin, Beauty and the Beast,*

Toy Story, Frozen, and *Princess Classics* and omnibus works such as *All Stars Carnival.*

· Please give one answer for each of these activities.

Items: Luxurious, Prestigious, High class

Choices: "1. Not applicable at all", "2. Not very applicable", "3. Neither", "4. Rather applicable" and "5. Very applicable."

6. Lexus / Daihatsu sponsors the Vienna Philharmonic Orchestra "Chamber Music Special" / Feld Entertainment "Disney On Ice." Please give one answer for each of these sponsorships.

Items: Luxurious, Prestigious, High class, Positive, Favorable, Good

Choices: "1. Not applicable at all", "2. Not very applicable", "3. Neither", "4. Rather applicable" and "5. Very applicable."

7. I would like to ask you again about Lexus/Daihatsu. Please give one answer for each of these brands.

Items: Positive, Favorable, Good

Choices: "1. Not applicable at all", "2. Not very applicable", "3. Neither", "4. Rather applicable" and "5. Very applicable."

8. We would like to ask you again about the Vienna Philharmonic Orchestra "Chamber Music Special" / Feld Entertainment "Disney On Ice." Please give one answer for each of these activities.

Items: Positive, Favorable, Good

Choices: "1. Not applicable at all", "2. Not very applicable", "3. Neither", "4. Rather applicable" and "5. Very applicable."

---

*We wrote this text by referring to Suntory Group (2018), which actually invited the Vienna Philharmonic Orchestra "Chamber Musical Special."

**We wrote this text by modifying the explanation of "Disney On Ice" on the website of Kyodo Tokyo. For each citation source, see the references.

SDGsを活用した新たな共通価値の創造（CSV）

笹谷　秀光

千葉商科大学基盤教育機構教授

キーワード：SDGs, CSV, 企業, 経営, 社会・環境課題, 経済価値, 事例分析, 統合要素

【要旨】

　社会課題への対応は多くの企業にとって経営上の重要命題となっている。マイケル・ポーターとマーク・クラマーは，社会・環境課題を解決しつつ経済価値の実現をねらうCSV（Creating Shared Value）を提唱したが，対象とする社会課題の洞察が十分でないなどの点が先行研究で指摘されている。現下の社会課題については，2015年に国連で策定された「持続可能な開発目標」（Sustainable Development Goals：SDGs）がある。本稿では，SDGs活用によりCSVの弱点を解決するSDGs/CSVの統合要素を提案し，事例によりその有効性を示す。

1. はじめに

　複雑化する社会課題解決への対応は，多くの企業にとって経営上の必須事項になっている。社会・環境課題を解決しつつ経済価値の実現もねらう企業戦略をマイケル・ポーターとマーク・クラマーがCreating Shared Value（CSV：共通価値の創造）と呼んだ（Porter and Kramer, 2011）。これは社会課題対処型の新たな経営戦略として先行研究でも評価され（赤池ら，2013および名和，2015ほか），CSV戦略を採用する日本企業も多い。

　しかしながら，CSVに関しては，①社会・環境課題の不明確性，②メソッドの弱さ，③発信面の弱点の指摘がある。

　一方，現下の社会課題に関しては，2015年に国連サミットで採択された文書 "Transforming our world: the 2030 agenda for sustainable development"[1]（邦訳は「我々の世界を変革する：持続可能な開発のための2030アジェンダ」（外務省仮訳，以下，「2030アジェンダ」という））[2]内の "Sustainable Development Goals：SDGs"（持続可能な開発目標）が有用である。これは社会課題に対処し持続可能な社会づくりを目指す2030年に向けた目標であり，社会課題を網羅的に提示しようとするものである。

　SDGsは企業に対し，本業に基づく創造性とイノベーションによりCSVを実現することを期待しており，SDGsができた今こそ，企業にとって競争優位につながるCSV推進ができると考える。

投稿論文（事例紹介・解説）（2020. 2.12受付／2020. 5.29受理）

著者は，先行研究で指摘されてきた，CSV の 3 つの弱点を解決するために，社会課題の国際的な共通言語である SDGs が活用できると考えた。そこで本稿では，まず，CSV の経営上の有用性と弱点について考察する。つぎに，SDGs を活用することで CSV の弱点を克服し，CSV を効果的に推進するための SDGs/CSV 統合要素を提案する。提案要素の有効性を示すために，SDGs を活用して CSV を展開している企業の事例を分析する。

2. | 研究の方法

まず，ポーターとクラマーの CSV 理論の有用性および弱点について確認する。つぎに，SDGs と，これを受けて，SDGs を企業経営に適用するための指針として発表された "SDGs Compass"（以下，「SDG コンパス」という）[3] についてレビューし，その特徴を整理する。次に，CSV と SDGs との関連について考察し，SDGs/CSV の統合要素を提示する。さらに，SDGs を活用した CSV の推進が CSV の弱点の克服につながることを実証するため，日本企業の SDGs を活用した CSV 事例を分析する。

これまで CSV と SDGs を関連づけて分析した日本企業に関する先行研究は少なく日本の事例を取り上げることは今後の日本企業のグローバルな経営戦略にとって重要な要素になりうると考える。

また，ポーターとクラマーによる CSV の 3 つの側面（①商品開発，②バリューチェーン，③産業クラスター）に即して，日本企業の SDGs 活用の事例を政府のジャパン SDGs アワード受賞者の中から，商品開発 CSV では第 1 回外務大臣賞のサラヤ株式会社[4]，バリューチェーン CSV では第 1 回特別賞の株式会社伊藤園[5] および産業クラスター CSV の事例として第 2

回特別賞の株式会社滋賀銀行[6] を選定する。これらの企業の SDGs 導入の効果を考察するため，SDGs を導入前の各社の状況と比較する。比較は各社の 2018 年統合報告書と SDGs 策定前の 2014 年の統合報告書または CSR 報告書での発信内容で行う。また，SDGs を導入していない事例として中堅飲料企業と地方銀行を匿名にて取り上げる。

3. | 結果

3-1. CSV 理論の進化過程と弱点の指摘

ポーターとクラマーの CSV には次の弱点が指摘されている。CSV は利益創出という経済的成功を達成する新しい方法であると示唆する一方で，企業の目的は利益創出そのものではなく共通価値の創造であると述べているなど，社会的価値の捉え方とメソッドに弱点がある（岡田，2012）。また，CSV は利益追求型のモデルから脱しておらず，いまや企業の志（パーパス）をしっかり示した新たな成長方法を探るべきである（名和，2015）として，CSV のメソッドと発信面での弱点を指摘する。そこで CSV について①社会課題の不明確性，②メソッドの弱さ，③発信力の弱さの 3 点の克服が論点である。

3-2. SDGs/CSV 統合要素

SDGs の企業向けの導入指針である SDG コンパスは，CSV が示す社会価値と経済価値の両立を意識してつくられている。SDGs の 17 目標は，企業にとってのチャンスである一方，リスク回避にも使えるリストであると捉えることが要点とされている。つまり，SDGs をこの両面でバランスよく使うことにより，チャンス面では他社より先駆けて社会課題対処を行い経済価値の実現と競争優位につなげることができ

る。一方，SDGs に示された社会課題解決とリスク回避を行えば社会価値の実現につながる。このようにチャンス面でもリスク回避面でもSDGs を活用することで社会課題が明確化されたCSV につながっていくと考えられる。

　SDGs の企業への導入指針である SDG コンパスは主として国際的企業向けにつくられているので，これを日本企業に当てはめる場合には日本ではこれまで「三方よし」のような社会との接点を意識した経営理念が多くみられることや地域にも貢献する長寿企業が多い一方，発信面ではグローバル企業に比べ必ずしも十分ではないなどの日本企業の特性も踏まえてローカライズ加工を行う必要がある。また，CSV の弱点の克服を念頭につくられたものではないので，この点に留意して SDG コンパスに加工を加える必要がある。さらに，SDG コンパス自体が国際的合意の下でできたものではないので，社会的責任の企業への導入については国際合意のある「社会的責任の手引」（ISO26000）の導入手順をベースにする必要がある（この点は別稿に譲る）。

　ここでは，CSV を進化させるには企業の志（パーパス）をしっかり示した新たな成長方法を探るべきである（名和，2015）との指摘を考慮しつつ SDG コンパスを参照する。

　そこで，SDG コンパスをそのまま使うのではなく企業に SDGs を導入していく 5 つのステップごとに CSV に関連づけ直し，特に企業のパーパスを示すことに関連するステップ 5 を改造強化する。この視点で，SDGs を CSV に生かすための要素を「SDGs/CSV 統合要素」としてまとめると，次のとおりである。

　　第 1 ステップ：SDGs を理解する
　　→要素 1：SDGs 活用による CSV の社会課題の客観化と社内共通認識の醸成

　　第 2 ステップ：優先課題を決定する
　　→要素 2：SDGs 活用による CSV の重点課題の抽出
　　第 3 ステップ：目標を設定する
　　→要素 3：SDGs に関連づけた目標設定と進行管理
　　第 4 ステップ：経営へ統合する
　　→要素 4：SDGs 活用による CSV 戦略の策定
　　第 5 ステップ：報告とコミュニケーションを行う
　　→要素 5：SDGs 活用による企業パーパスの発信

　この中で，発信面ではグローバル企業に比べ必ずしも十分ではないなどの日本企業の特性とCSV の弱点の一つである発信性のあいまいさを補完し，企業のパーパスを強く打ち出すために，要素 5 を補強する。そうすれば，図 1 で示すように，SDGs により，CSV が解決しようとする社会課題が客観化し，SDG コンパスの援用で CSV のメソッド性の弱さを補完できる。加えて，SDGs の世界共通言語としての発信性の強さから企業のパーパスが明確化する。この結果，いわば，「進化型 CSV」につながると考える。

3-3. CSV 事例の分析―SDGs/CSV 統合要素との関連

　この SDGs/CSV 統合要素を使って，CSV の 3 つの側面の事例について SDGs 活用の効果，特に，企業パーパスの訴求力に着目して事例分析した結果は，次のとおりである。

（1）　商品開発の CSV（サラヤ）

　サラヤは，ウガンダとカンボジアで，自社の消毒剤活用という事業を通じて，手洗いを基本とする衛生の向上のための取り組みを推進して

図1　SDGs/CSV 統合要素と統合の効果

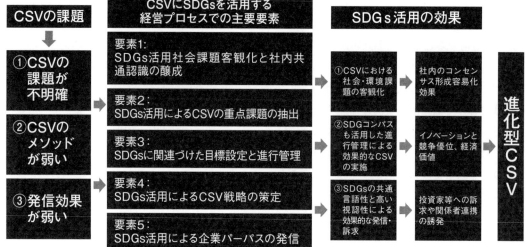

出所：筆者作成。

いる。「100万人の手洗いプロジェクト」として，対象製品の売上1％を，ウガンダにおけるユニセフの手洗い普及活動を支援。ウガンダに「現地法人サラヤ・イーストアフリカ」を設立し，現地生産の消毒剤やその使用方法を含めた衛生マニュアルを提供。持続可能なパーム油類（RSPO認証油）の使用や，アブラヤシ生産地の生物多様性の保全に取り組むと同時に，消費者へのエシカル消費の啓発も実施している。

　SDGs/CSV 統合要素からみれば，要素1の課題把握ではトップから社員までの理解の浸透が進んでおり，SDGs との関連では，貢献しているSDGs目標3（健康），目標6（水とトイレ），目標12（つくる責任つかう責任）を軸にして，目標14（陸上資源），目標15（海洋資源）にもつなげている。要素2の重点課題の選定は終わっており，新たに，SDGs-ESG の観点から深めてサラヤ基本理念を踏まえた「サステナビリティ推進方針」を制定し（2019年11月8日），重要課題への取り組みを明示した。要素3の目標設定では的確に進行管理し，経時的に結果報告を行う。要素4では，経営資源配分面

でも，同社の中長期計画やトップメッセージでSDGs を主軸に位置づけている。

　要素5の企業パーパスの訴求面では，「サラヤ持続可能性レポート2019」で「サラヤのサプライチェーンを通した取り組みにおけるSDGs の目標とターゲットのフロー」としてすべてターゲットレベルでSDGs との紐づけを示している。トップが主導し，更家悠介社長はサラヤの活動では，利益優先でなく，環境，自然に配慮した商品を出すことおよび世界的な環境保全や貧困対策などの社会貢献をすることの2点を強調し，企業パーパスを発信している。

　サラヤは，SDGs 導入前の2014年レポートでは，2000年の国連ミレニアム宣言に基づくミレニアム開発目標（MDGs）への言及はあるものの，社会課題への対処について本業というよりは社会貢献的な位置づけで紹介していた。サラヤでのSDGs への言及は早く，すでに2015年秋発行の2015年レポートで，2015年9月に採択予定のSDGs に対しても，ビジネスを通じて実践を図っていきたいと述べ，その前にサラヤのMDGs の総括をしており先駆的で

あった。サラヤは非上場であるが，SDGs に関する情報開示が進んだ結果，内外で幅広く通用する SDGs 経営の代表的事例となっている。同社の「100 万人の手洗いプロジェクト」などが評価され，ウガンダ共和国サム・カハンバ・クテサ外務大臣より更家悠介社長が「ウガンダ共和国名誉領事」に任命された。あわせてサラヤ本町ビル内に在大阪名誉領事館を開設した。SDGs 導入後は格段に企業パーパスの対外訴求力が増し，SDGs アワード外務大臣賞に結びついている。

（2）　バリューチェーンの CSV（伊藤園）

伊藤園は，バリューチェーンを見直し，農業課題を解決する「茶産地育成事業」に取り組んでいる。

SDGs/CSV 統合要素からみれば，要素1と要素2では，SDGs 目標2（持続可能な農業），目標8（成長・雇用）および目標9（イノベーション）につながり，目標11（持続可能な都市）の地域社会活性化にも寄与し，行政・農業者との目標17（パートナーシップ）で実現している。同社は SDGs 推進方針を定め，要素3，4の内容を社内外にコミットしている。とくに要素5では，SDGs を関係者に伝わりやすい形で統合報告書などで発信している。同社の CSV は，ポーターの名前にちなんだポーター賞（一橋大学大学院運営）の受賞（2013 年）以降進化し，現在は SDGs/CSV 統合要素を経営に生かしている代表事例となっている。同社では SDGs 導入後は，社内モチベーション向上も図られた。CSV における社会課題がより明確化され対外訴求力が高まり，アワード特別賞受賞に結びついた。持続可能な生産と消費という企業のパーパスが伝わった結果である。

2014 年のレポートでは CSV を全面的に打ち出しているが，社会課題については一般的に述べるにとどまっており，企業パーパスの訴求力の点で SDGs 導入後とは大きな違いがある。

中堅飲料企業 A 社は ESG に力を注ぎ，社会・環境活動も多く行っているが，SDGs への言及はほとんどないので，SDGs 経営のような発信性は今のところ見られない。

（3）　産業クラスターの CSV（滋賀銀行）

滋賀銀行の「行是」（1966 年制定）は近江商人の経営哲学である「三方よし」の精神を原点としたものとなっている。SDGs が策定されると，ただちに，地域経済，地球環境，人材の三本柱からなる「しがぎん SDGs 宣言」を発出し，関係者と連携した地域づくりに向けた地域クラスターの CSV を促している。

SDGs/CSV 統合要素からみれば，要素1では，「しがぎん SDGs 宣言」に基づき，関係者間ネットワークを使い，SDGs の実践について取引先企業などに指導的役割を発揮している。要素2では，金融業の本業である融資に SDGs を加味した商品開発を行い，融資ノウハウを生かした関係者とのネットワークづくりも行う。また，銀行内での働き方や ICT 化などの改革でも SDGs が重点課題である。要素3の目標設定も的確に行っている。要素4では，「しがぎん SDGs 宣言」に即して SDGs 経営を目指している。

要素5では，2030 年のマイルストーン（ターゲット 2030）という形で，地域経済の創造，地球環境の持続性，多様な人材の育成の3点で経済・環境・人をつなぐこと（統合的発展）を目指している。経済的価値と社会的価値を両立することで地域社会の発展に取り組むこととし，すべて SDGs と関連づけて，企業パーパスを効果的に発信している。

同行の 2019 年 CSR レポートでは，高橋正一郎頭取より「当行の取り組みは国連が提唱する SDGs と同じ視線を持って」おり，「経済的価値と社会的価値を創造し，両立させて『共有価

図2　SDGs/CSV 統合要素と事例分析・統合の効果

SDGs/CSVの5つの統合要素		サラヤ 導入以前	サラヤ SDGs導入	伊藤園 導入以前	伊藤園 SDGs導入	A社（飲料）未導入	滋賀銀行 導入以前	滋賀銀行 SDG導入	B社（地銀）未導入	SDGs/CSV統合の効果	
CSVの課題 ①CSVの課題が不明確	SDGsによる社会課題の明確化とCSVの類型	独自の発信（MDGsについては言及）	SDGs3、6、17、12、14、15（消毒剤の吸収還事業化・新市場開拓）商品開発CSV	独自の発信 ボジョーター賞を受賞	SDGs2、8、9、11、17（緑 収益化：調達安定）バリューチェーンCSV	独自の発信、ESGには力を注ぐ 社会課題解決による価値創造には言及	熱心に課環の共存やCSR活動を推進	SDGs17 地域社会との共創 環境関連の地域クラスターCSV	独自の発信	①CSVにおける社会・環境課題の客観化	形成社内の容易化コンセンサス効果
②CSVのメソッドが弱い	統合要素1：SDGs活用による社会課題抽出と社内共通認識の醸成	社内は必ずしも理解浸透せず	衛生マニュアル提供で社内意識統一	社内は必ずしも理解浸透せず	推進方針をつくり社内意識醸成	SDGsには言及せず	CSR方針は定めていた	「しがぎんSDGs宣言」で意識統一	社内は必ずしも理解浸透せず	②SDGsコンパスを活用した進行構築・管理・戦略構築・関係者連携による効果的なCSVの実施	競争優位と経済価値
	統合要素2：SDGs活用による課題の重点抽出	関係者とは連携	ウガンダに現地法人つくり連携	関係者とは連携	行政・農業者と連携	関係者とは連携	関係者とは連携	地域関係企業と連携	関係者とは連携		
	統合要素3：SDGsに関連付けたCSVの重点目標設定と進行管理	特になし	体制整備しPDCA	特になし	担当役員も定めPDCA	特になし	特になし	推進責任者を決めPDCA	特になし		
③発信効果が弱い	統合要素4：SDGs活用によるCSV戦略の策定	特になし	中長期明計画に明記	特になし	SDGs推進方針を役員会決定	特になし	特になし	中長期計画に明記	特になし	③SDGsの共通言語性と高い視認性による効果的な発信・訴求	連携・訴求投資家等の関係者への誘因発信
	統合要素5：SDGs活用による企業パーパスの発信	左ほど発信性なし	アワード受賞で発信強化	左ほど発信性なし	世界雑誌「フォーチュン」	発信性は強くない	外部への発信の強化を促す意見	トップからの発信	発信性は強くない		

SDGsによる客観化と経済価値の実現につながるCSV

値』を生み出し，地域社会の発展に尽力」する
として CSV も明示している。同行が目指す姿
を「Sustainability Design Company」と表現
し SDGs をビジョンの中に取り込んでいる。
SDGs 導入以前には，滋賀銀行の 2015 CSR レ
ポートでは，龍谷大学社会学部教授長・上深雪
氏から第三者意見として関係者に「知らせてい
く」取り組みの強化の必要性が指摘されてい
た。

　また，滋賀銀行は 2019 年 5 月に地銀 8 行で
つくる「TSUBASA アライアンス」に参加し
た。参加は，千葉銀行，第四銀行，中国銀行，
伊予銀行，東邦銀行，北洋銀行，北越銀行，武
蔵野銀行に加え，9 行となる。これを契機に，
TSUBASA アライアンスは，SDGs を踏まえた
「TSUBASA SDGs 宣言」を制定した。今後，
SDGs アワード受賞企業の滋賀銀行の参加でそ
のノウハウの水平展開が図られることも明らか
となった。

　一方，同じく地方銀行の B 社では，統合報
告書ではなく環境報告書を発行しているが，そ
の中で，SDGs への言及はあるが環境計画の中
への位置づけとなっており SDGs 経営にはなっ
ていないので，訴求力が高くない。

4.　考察

4-1.　CSV 事例分析と SDGs/CSV 統合要素の有効性

　企業の CSV 事例について，「SDGs/CSV 統
合要素」の各要素別に検証し統合要素の効果を
検証した結果を，先に示した図 1 の中心部に事
例の分析表を掲げたものが図 2 である。図左に
掲げた前述の CSV の 3 つの弱点について，
CSV を SDGs と統合することで克服を目指す。
弱点①については SDGs を当てはめることで，
世界共通言語としての社会・環境課題に対処し

ていることが明確になる。SDGs 導入前の状況
や未導入のケースでは，独自に社会課題の説明
をしなければならず，課題についての客観性が
弱い。SDGs を使えば社内コンセンサスの形成
や社外発信での訴求力が強くなる。弱点②につ
いては，SDG コンパスを使うことで要素 2，要
素 3，要素 4 といった重要なプロセスにおいて
具体的メソッドを提供するので，これを使え
ば，CSV のメソッドの弱さを補強できる。
SDGs 導入企業は，これをうまく活用している
一方，導入前・未導入の企業ではこの効果がな
いので独自にプロセスを考慮する必要がある。
弱点③の CSV の発信に関しては，要素 5 で，
SDGs 導入企業はグローバルに企業パーパスの
発信を強め，アワード受賞企業はさらにその発
信力を高めている。

　このように，SDGs/CSV 統合という方法を
とることにより，図 2 に記載したとおり，CSV
の 3 つの弱点を克服しつつ，図の右に示した通
り，次の統合効果が生ずる。第一に，CSV に
おける社会・環境課題が客観化し，社内のコン
センサス形成容易化効果が生まれる。第二に，
対外的にはイノベーションと競争優位による経
済価値の創出に結びつき，CSV の本来的ねら
いを達成できる。第三に SDGs による効果的な
発信は，投資家等への好影響やさらなる関係者
連携の誘発につながる。以上から，SDGs によ
り客観化された社会課題の解決と経済価値の同
時実現につながる CSV となる。その結果とし
て，企業のパーパスを明確に世界に発信できる
効果を享受している。このように SDGs/CSV
統合要素は CSV の進化と企業パーパスの訴求
に役立つものである。

4-2.　CSV を進化させる SDGs

　以上の SDGs/CSV 統合要素についての分析
から，次のことがわかる。まず，SDGs を活用

することにより，どの社会課題に対処している CSV なのかが内外に伝わり，CSV の弱点とされる社会課題について客観性を持たせることができる。SDGs と関連づけなければどのような課題に対処しているのかはそれぞれ個別に工夫して伝える必要があるが，SDGs を使えば共通言語での発信となるという特性から，自社の CSV のねらいが効果的に伝わりやすい。SDGs の網羅性と認知しやすい特徴から，CSV のストーリーテリングの質を向上させることにつながっている。

　加えて，SDGs を共通言語として使用することで，取引先や NGO/NPO などとの目的の共有ができ，国際的競争に打ち勝つ能力を高める効果が期待できる。関係者との連携も深まり，社会課題解決型のイノベーションが生まれることが期待できる。サラヤでは進出先国との協調，伊藤園では行政・農業者との協働，滋賀銀行では関係企業との連携が生まれている。加えて，社員が社会課題解決に寄与していることが客観的にわかるので，CSV を通じ社員モチベーションを向上させることができる。サラヤ，伊藤園での方針策定や滋賀銀行の「しがぎん SDGs 宣言」はこの効果を強めている。

　以上から，SDGs/CSV 統合要素は，企業価値の向上，関係者連携と社員モチベーション向上に効果があり，SDGs で CSV を進化させることができることが明らかになった。

5. ｜ おわりに

　本稿では，CSV の弱点を克服するために，SDG コンパスをカスタマイズし，CSV を進化させ企業のパーパスを明示するための SDGs/CSV 統合要素を提案した。SDG コンパスはこのようにカスタマイズして使えば CSV が示す社会課題の解決と企業の経済利益の両立に役立

ち，この SDGs/CSV 統合要素は，CSV の弱点を克服するための有用なツールになりうることが明らかになった。

　今後，これらの SDGs/CSV 統合要素を分析ツールとして，幅広い事例分析を通じた，「SDGs/CSV 統合経営モデル」といった形でモデルを形成することが重要課題の一つであり，今後さらに深耕していきたい。

(1)　United Nations (2015) 'Transforming our world: the 2030 agenda for sustainable development', 70th session of the United Nations General Assembly; 2015.9.25; New York.（Resolution A/RES/70/1), Available at http://www.un.org/ga/search/view_doc.asp?symbol=A/RES/70/1&Lang=E, Accessed April 1st 2020.

(2)　外務省「我々の世界を変革する：持続可能な開発のための 2030 アジェンダ（外務省仮訳）」, Available at https://www.mofa.go.jp/mofaj/files/000101402.pdf, Accessed April 1st 2020.

(3)　SDG Compass, https://sdgcompass.org/, Accessed April 1st 2020.

(4)　サラヤ, https://www.saraya.com/, Accessed April 1st 2020.

(5)　伊藤園, https://www.itoen.co.jp/, Accessed April 1st 2020.

(6)　滋賀銀行, https://www.shigagin.com/, Accessed April 1st 2020.

〈参考文献〉
Porter, M.E. and Kramer, M.R. (2002) 'The Competitive Advantage of Corporate Philanthropy', *Harvard Business Review*, Vol. 80, No. 12, pp. 56-68.
── and Kramer, M.R. (2006) 'Strategy and Society: The Link Between Competitive Advantage and Corporate Social Responsibility', *Harvard Business Review*, Vol. 84, No. 12, pp. 78-92.
── and Kramer, M.R. (2011) 'Creating Shared Value', *Harvard Business Review*, Vol. 89, Issue 1/2, pp. 62-77.
赤池学・水上武彦（2013）『CSV 経営─社会的課題の解決と事業を両立する』NTT 出版。
岡田正大（2012）「戦略理論の体系と「共有価値」概念がもたらす理論的影響について」，『慶應経営論集』，第 29 巻第 1 号，pp. 121-139。
佐藤憲正・中山健・百武仁志（2013）「自由論題（43）

日本企業の競争力と CSV」『経営学論集第 84 集』，pp.(43)1-12。

笹谷秀光（2019a)「持続可能性新時代におけるグローバル競争戦略―SDGs 活用による新たな価値創造―」第 70 回全国能率大会懸賞論文，Available at https://www.zen-noh-ren.or.jp/conference/article-list/，Accessed June 1st 2019.

――（2019b)「『SDGs 経営』の 5 要素と発信のための SDGs 対応マトリックスの開発」，『千葉商科大学 PSR』，No. 47, pp. 31-41。

――（2019c)『Q & A SDGs 経営』，日本経済新聞出版社。

名和高司（2015)『CSV 経営戦略―本業での高収益と，社会の課題を同時に解決する』，東洋経済新報社。

――（2018)『企業変革の教科書』，東洋経済新報社。

学会ニュース

1. 第 9 回年次大会（2019 年 9 月 5〜6 日）報告
2. 部会（2019 年 12 月〜2020 年 5 月）報告
3. 第 10 回年次大会（2021 年 9 月）案内

1. 第 9 回年次大会（2019 年 9 月 5〜6 日）報告

- ・日　　　程　　2019 年 9 月 5 日（木）〜6 日（金）
- ・場　　　所　　早稲田大学早稲田キャンパス 14 号館 4 階
- ・主　　　催　　企業と社会フォーラム
- ・協　　　力　　B Corp Asia，凸版印刷
- ・本大会プログラム委員会

　　　　　　福川恭子（一橋大学大学院教授）

　　　　　　Schmidpeter, René (Professor, Cologne Business School, Germany)

　　　　　　谷本寛治（早稲田大学教授）

- ・テ ー マ　　「サステナビリティ人材の育成と経営教育」

　　過去 20 年間において CSR は重要な経営課題，そして研究・教育課題として広がり，新しいマインドセットをもった研究者や実務家の育成が求められています。サステナビリティという概念は，ビジネス界においてますます重要になってきているにもかかわらず，企業がグローバルな社会的課題に取り組むことには無理があると長らく考えられてきました。しかしながら，今やビジネスや NGO の現場において，サステナビリティ・マインドをもった人材の育成が求められています。サステナビリティは経営のあり方や教育に新しいビジョンを提示していくポテンシャルを秘めており，従来のマネジメントスキルの教育にとどまらず，幅広く社会との議論を行っていくことが期待されています。CSR，サステナビリティの課題に取り組んでいくには，現代の複雑な課題や議論にトータルにアプローチする視点が求められています。サステナビリティへの関心の高まりは，大学・ビジネススクールに実務界から責任あるリーダーシップと高い倫理意識をもった卒業生を育てることが期待されています。ビジネス教育の国際認証 AACSB では，今や各ビジネススクールにその教育・研究において CSR 関連の課題に取り組むことを求めています。ただこれらのことは日本ではまだあまり理解されていません。CSR/サステナビリティ教育は，大学と企業，国際機関，NGO などが協力しながら取り組まれ，ローカル/グローバルな課題の解決に貢献していく人材を育成していくことが期待されています。

　　2019 年 JFBS 年次大会では，大学や現場におけるこれまでとこれからの議論や事例をもとに，CSR やサステナビリティ経営教育を取り巻く問題や新しい可能性について多様な観点から議論しました。

・プログラム

＜大会1日目：2019年9月5日＞

10:30-11:30	JFBS 理事会
11:30-12:00	JFBS 総会
12:00-13:00	受付
13:00-13:10	**Opening Remarks** ・Kanji Tanimoto (Waseda University, Japan / Japan Forum of Business and Society)
13:10-14:40	**Keynote Speech** ・Toshio Arima (Global Compact Network Japan, Japan) 　"Business and SDGs" ・Elisabeth Fröhlich (Cologne Business School, Germany) 　"The Necessity of Sustainability in Management Education" 【Chair】Kanji Tanimoto (Waseda University, Japan)
14:40-14:50	コーヒーブレイク
14:50-16:15	**Plenary Session 1 "CSR/Sustainability in Management Education"** ・Toshio Arima (Global Compact Network Japan, Japan) ・Elisabeth Fröhlich (Cologne Business School, Germany) ・Takayuki Kitajima (Unilever Japan Holdings, Japan) ・Michele John (Curtin University, Australia) 【Chair】Kyoko Fukukawa (Hitotsubashi University, Japan)
16:15-16:30	コーヒーブレイク
16:30-18:00	**Breakout Session Organized 1「企業における『ビジネスと人権』教育・研修の課題」** ・菊池浩（法務省） ・齊藤誠（ビジネスと人権ロイヤーズネットワーク） ・杉本茂（ANA ホールディングス） 【司会】足達英一郎（日本総合研究所） **Session 1 (CFP) "Sustainability in Management Education 1"** 1. Alicia SM Leung and Yu Ha Cheung (Hong Kong Baptist University, Hong Kong) 　"Designing an Integrative Sustainability Management Curriculum" 2. Miriam Garvi (National Taiwan University, Taiwan) 　Ariana Chang (Fu Jen Catholic University, Taiwan) 　Corey Lien (B Lab Taiwan, Taiwan) 　"B Corps in the Classroom-Approaches to Responsible Management Education in Taiwan" 【Chair】Michele John (Curtin University, Australia) **Session 2 (CFP) Organized by B Corp Asia** 1. Nirawat Thammajak (Suranaree University of Technology, Thailand) 　"The Role of Science and Innovation Park in Promoting University's Social Responsibility" 2. Supree Baosingsauy (Charoen Pokphand for Rural Lives' Development Foundation, Thailand) 　"Social Enterprise Practice Integrated to Community Development Through School Lunch Project & Local Store/Market Move to Community-Based Tourism (Social

	Business)" 3. Sirikul Laukaikul (Sustainable Brand Bangkok, Thailand) "Sufficiency Economy and Sustainable Brand" 4. Trin Thananusak (Mahidol University, Thailand) "Sustainability in Management Education: The Case of College of Management, Mahidol University and The Collaborations with External Bodies"
	Session 3 (CFP) Doctoral Workshop 1. 吉田賢一（早稲田大学） 「企業不祥事（リコール）後の市場の反応：CSR 活動が与える影響」 2. Nathania A. Chua, Josep F. Mària and Ignasi L. Martí (ESADE, Universitat Ramon Llull, Spain) "Transformative Experiences in Service-Learning" 3. Miho Murashima (Waseda University, Japan) "Does Corporate Social Responsibility Raise Investors' Assessment of a Firm and Its Value in Japan?" 【Mentor】Elisabeth Fröhlich (Cologne Business School, Germany) Kyoko Fukukawa (Hitotsubashi University, Japan) Kanji Tanimoto (Waseda University, Japan)
18:00-18:30	休憩・移動
18:30-20:00	交流会（於早稲田キャンパス・レストラン「森の風」）

＜大会 2 日目：2019 年 9 月 6 日＞

9:00-10:30	**Breakout Session Organized 2 "Sustainability Leadership Training"** ・Gefei Yin (GoldenBee Corporate Social Responsibility Consulting, China) ・Masahiro Okada (Keio University, Japan) ・Tomoko Hasegawa (Keidanren, Japan Business Federation, Japan) 【Chair】Masao Seki (Sompo Japan Nipponkoa Insurance, Japan)
	Session4 (CFP)「日本企業の CSR 経営」 1. 森翔人（The Global Alliance for Sustainable Supply Chain） 　土肥将敦（法政大学） 「持続可能なサプライチェーンの構築に向けて―労働者へのエンパワメントを通じた新たなモニタリングモデルの提案―」 2. 芳賀和恵（文京学院大学） 「高齢化社会における人材教育の課題：企業の人材教育と大学の生涯教育の補完的関係の可能性の検討」 3. 池内博一（追手門学院大学） 「従業員の不適切行為と企業の事前・事後対策―従業員に対する法的責任追及と従業員教育―」 【司会】古村公久（京都産業大学）
	Session 5 (CFP) Part 1 B Corp Special Session: Global B Corp Movement and Asia Development "Using Business as a Force for Good, unleash the DNA within" ・Ariana Chang (Fu Jen Catholic University, Taiwan) ・Corey Lien (B Corp Asia)

	・Ken Ito (Asian Venture Philanthropy Network) ・Sakulthip Keeratiphantawong (NISE Corporation / B Corp Thailand)
10:30-10:50	コーヒーブレイク
10:50-12:20	**Breakout Session Organized 3 "Higher Education for Sustainability"** ・Akiko Imai (Showa Women's University, Japan) ・Joel Malen (Waseda University, Japan) ・Philip Sugai (Doshisha University, Japan) ・Yoshiteru Uramoto (Sophia University, Japan) 【Chair】Hiroshi Amemiya (Arabesque S-Ray GmbH Japan branch, Japan)
	Session 5 (CFP) Part 2 B Corp Special Session: Global B Corp Movement and Asia Development ditto
	Session 6 (CFP) "Sustainability in Management Education 2" 1. ABM Shahidul Islam and Jahan Ruma Akhtar Shirin (Center for Promoting Global Education, Bangladesh) 　Forhad Hossain (LBS Management Consultancy, Bangladesh) 　"Study on Adaptation of Corporate Social Responsibility in Academic Education in Bangladesh" 2. Michele John, Samad Suleman and Adriel Ichawat (Curtin University, Australia) 　"Sustainability in Engineering Education in Australia-Challenges and Learnings" 【Chair】Chi-Jui Huang (National Taipei University, Taiwan)
12:20-13:20	昼食
13:20-14:50	**Breakout Session Organized 4「サステナビリティ人材の育成におけるメディアの役割」** ・木幡美子（フジテレビジョン） ・倉持裕和（朝日新聞社） ・堅達京子（NHK エンタープライズ） 【司会】牛島慶一（EY 新日本有限責任監査法人）
	Session 7 (CFP) "CSR Management 1" 1. Chi-Jui Huang and Wen-Chyan Ke (National Taipei University, Taiwan) 　Meng Ju Kao (National Taiwan University, Taiwan) 　"Does Materiality of CSR Matter for Financial Performance?" 2. Sung-Min Lin (National Chung-Hsing University, Taiwan) 　Yen-Ching Liu (National Yunlin University of Science and Technology, Taiwan) 　"Challenges of Middle Managers in Embedding CSR into Therapeutic Industry-An Illustration of Managerial Strategies based on the Leadership Theory, and Distributed Theory in the Process of Coordinating Investigational New Drug Development" 【Chair】Megumi Suto (Waseda University, Japan)
	Session 8 (CFP) "CSR Management 2" 1. Meng-Ying Tsai (Zhaoqing University, China) 　Wan-Chi Hsu (Lee-Ming Institute of Technology, Taiwan) 　"Corporate Social Responsibility Perception, Job Satisfaction and Organization Commitment: Evidence from Five-Star Hotel in China" 2. Retna Rehajeng (Soka University, Japan)

	"CSR Management Practice in an Asian Developing Countries: Indonesian Case" 【Chair】 Joel Malen (Waseda University, Japan)
14:50–15:10	休憩
15:10–16:30	**Plenary Session 2 "Wrap-up Session: CSR/Sustainability in Management Education"** ・Masao Seki (Sompo Japan Nipponkoa Insurance, Japan) ・Hiroshi Amemiya (Arabesque S-Ray GmbH Japan branch, Japan) ・Keiichi Ushijima (Ernst & Young ShinNihon, Japan) 【Chair】 Kyoko Fukukawa (Hitotsubashi University, Japan)
16:30–16:40	**Closing Remarks** ・Kanji Tanimoto (Waseda University, Japan / Japan Forum of Business and Society)
16:40–18:00	フェアウエルドリンク

2. 部会報告

第30回東日本部会
　・日　時　2019年12月14日（土）13：30〜17：00
　・場　所　早稲田大学早稲田キャンパス11号館8階803教室
　・テーマ・報告者等
　(1) NGOキャンペーンと市場へのインパクト
　　　【報告者】小野美和氏（立教大学ビジネスデザイン研究科（院））
　(2) サーキュラーエコノミーへ向けて―企業実践事例の紹介―
　　　【報告者】今津秀紀氏（凸版印刷トッパンアイデアセンター）
　(3) 学界展望
　　　【報告者】谷本寛治教授（早稲田大学商学学術院商学部）
　　　【司　会】谷本寛治教授（早稲田大学商学学術院商学部）

第31回東日本部会
　2020年5月23日（土）に開催予定であったが，新型コロナウイルス感染症の影響により中止となった。

3. 第10回年次大会（2021年9月）案内

・日　　程　　2021年9月初旬
　　　　　　　※2020年9月4〜5日に開催予定であったが，新型コロナウイルス感染症の影響により1
　　　　　　　年延期となった。
・場　　所　　早稲田大学早稲田キャンパス
・参 加 者　　JFBS会員および非会員（国内外の学界，産業界，労働界，NPO/NGO，学生など）
・テ ー マ　　「サーキュラーエコノミーを目指して」

　　生産―消費―廃棄，これは伝統的な産業モデルであり，これまでほとんどのビジネスは
このモデルで行われてきました。しかしこの直線的なモデルはもはや持続可能ではありま
せん。Ellen MacArthur Foundationなどは，資源やエネルギー消費と経済成長を切り離
し，実行可能で再生可能な循環型経済（サーキュラーエコノミー）を提唱しています。サー
キュラーエコノミーでは，廃棄物となったものが他のバリューチェーンの資源となること，
生産から消費そして廃棄に至るまでの商品ライフサイクルのすべての段階で，いま使われ
ているものを最大限利用していこうとしています。

　　サーキュラーエコノミーのビジネスモデルに関する文献では，廃棄物のリサイクル戦略
（循環をつくる）や商品寿命を伸ばすためのエコ開発（循環のスピードを緩める）が多く論
じられてきました。また高い耐久性による消費サイクルの長期化，所有に代わって必要な
時に利用することや，デジタルプラットフォームを通じた商品の再循環の支援といったシェ
アリングエコノミーのように，従来とは異なる方法によって循環スピードを緩めることが
議論されています。

　　世界が直面している危機的な気候変動や資源不足のもと，各国では循環型の事業イニシ
アティブを活性化させ，直線的なモデルを一部の戦略的なものに限定し，サーキュラーエ
コノミーへ移行することを促す法規制づくりが進められています。

　　2021年JFBS年次大会では，サーキュラーエコノミーの理論構築に向けた議論を進めて
いきます。サーキュラーエコノミーはどのように周辺の概念やパラダイム，例えばサステ
ナビリティや産業エコロジー（産業における資源やエネルギーの流れ），パーマカルチャー
（持続可能な農業・文化），シェアリングエコノミーに影響を及ぼすのか？われわれは，サー
キュラーエコノミーにかかわるテーマを学際的に考えるとともに，これまでのそしてこれ
からの議論と具体的な取り組みについて考えていきます。主に以下のようなトピックが挙
げられます（但しこの限りではありません）。

1. サーキュラーエコノミーにかかわる政策と戦略。サーキュラーエコノミーへの移行はど
　　のような規制や制度によって可能になるか？どのような公共政策が地域レベル，国家レ
　　ベル，国際レベルでサーキュラーエコノミーの発展を促すか？企業はどのようにサーキュ
　　ラーエコノミーの概念を戦略に組み込んでいくのか？
2. サーキュラーエコノミーを促進する企業家精神。サーキュラーエコノミーの分野におけ
　　る企業家精神とは何か？彼らは地域，国家，国際的にどのようにサーキュラーエコノミー
　　に取り組んでいるのか？
3. 新しい消費パターンとサーキュラーエコノミー。サーキュラーエコノミーの発展に向け
　　た消費者の行動やモチベーションについて。
4. 関連テーマとして，サステナブル・ファッション，食品ロス，プラスチック問題への取
　　り組み，シェアリング（車，自転車，場所など），持続可能な農業，再生可能エネルギー

　　　　などについて。

　　　　　多くの参加者の皆様によって新しい議論が提起されることを期待しています。

・企画セッション　　・廃プラスチック問題への取り組み

　　　　　　　　　　・食品ロス問題への取り組み

　　　　　　　　　　・サステナブル・ファッション

最新の詳細プログラムは，学会ウエブサイトを参照ください。

https://j-fbs.jp/annualconf_2021.html

【Notes for Contributors】

1. The annals mainly consists of invited paper, research paper and case study/general review. For submission to the annals, membership requirement does not apply.

2. Contributions should be original papers written in either Japanese or English on the theme of the JFBS annual conference in that year or topics related to business and society. The contributions have neither been published previously nor are under review for publication elsewhere by the end of September when the annals comes out.

3. Japan Forum of Business and Society (JFBS) has all copyrights of submitted papers for publication.

4. Authors are requested to seek written permission in advance when citing their accepted papers in any other publication including internet sites. With the request accepted, authors cite the annals information such as the series number and the date of publication.

5. All papers are to be submitted in a single column format. Research paper in Japanese language should be no longer than 20,000 characters (case study/general review: 10,000 characters) including title, abstract, keywords, notes, references, tables and figures. Research paper in English should be no longer than 8,000-11,000 words (case study/general review: 4,000-6,000 words) including title, abstract, keywords, notes, references, tables and figures.

6. References should be cited in the text either in brackets, e.g. *Earlier studies (Schumpeter, 1934) showed*⋯or as part of a sentence, e.g. *Schumpeter (1934) states*⋯. The reference should be listed alphabetically in the end of papers. In submitted papers, authors should not cite their own previous papers.

7. Authors should attach a cover letter which includes the title of the paper, author(s)' name(s), author(s)' contact information, an abstract (100 to 150 words) and keywords (10 words or phrases) in a word format.

8. Authors should follow the guidelines posted at the JFBS site to ensure their submission is in the correct format. (It is particularly important that authors may not use any third-party material such as figures and images on the internet and photos without appropriate permissions.)

9. Submission deadline for the research paper and case study/general review is the end of January after the annual conference, and for the invited paper, the end of March.

10. The annals uses a double-blind peer review system, in which two referees delegated by the JFBS editorial committee review. Then, the chief editor makes a final decision.

11. When accepted, authors can proofread for publication only once. Neither adding nor deleting sentences/ words can be made while proofreading. Only typographical/literal errors could be corrected.

12. All materials along with submitted papers are not returned to authors for any reason.

13. Papers should be submitted in a word file to info@j-fbs.jp
    Tel & Fax: +81-3-3203-7132   E-mail: info@j-fbs.jp   URL: https://j-fbs.jp
    Japan Forum of Business and Society (JFBS)
    c/o: Tanimoto Office, School of Commerce, Waseda University,
    1-6-1 Nishiwaseda, Shinjyuku-Ku, Tokyo 169-8050, Japan

Japan Forum of Business and Society Annals, No.9

CSR/Sustainability in Management Education

Edited by Japan Forum of Business and Society
Published by Chikura Publishing

Index

企業と社会フォーラム学会誌

サステナビリティ人材の育成と経営教育
【企業と社会シリーズ9】

2020年9月1日　発行

編　者　企業と社会フォーラム

発行者　千倉成示

発行所　株式会社　千倉書房
　　　　〒104-0031　東京都中央区京橋2-4-12
　　　　Tel 03-3273-3931　Fax 03-3273-7668
　　　　https://www.chikura.co.jp/

印刷／製本　藤原印刷

表紙デザイン　さくらい　ともか